WITNESS
IN
SIX CONTINENTS

WITNESS
IN
SIX CONTINENTS

Records of the Meeting of the
Commission on World Mission and Evangelism
of the
World Council of Churches
held in Mexico City
December 8th to 19th, 1963

Edited by

RONALD K. ORCHARD

Published for the

DIVISION OF WORLD MISSION AND EVANGELISM
OF THE WORLD COUNCIL OF CHURCHES

by

EDINBURGH HOUSE PRESS
1964

Edinburgh House Press
2 Eaton Gate, London, S.W.1

First published 1964

266
WOR

35466

MADE AND PRINTED IN GREAT BRITAIN BY
MORRISON AND GIBB LIMITED
LONDON AND EDINBURGH

Contents

T<small>HE</small> meeting of the Commission on World Mission and Evangelism held in Mexico City in December 1963 was the first full meeting of the Commission following the integration of the International Missionary Council and the World Council of Churches at New Delhi in 1961. The meeting of the Commission in New Delhi immediately following the Assemblies of the International Missionary Council and the World Council of Churches at which their integration was completed was a brief one dealing largely with formal matters. The meeting in Mexico was thus the first occasion at which a fully representative meeting of the Commission had met to consider its responsibilities, review its work and determine the lines of its future policy and activities. It therefore marked a significant point both in the development of ecumenical organization and in the thought and action of Churches and missionary agencies.

The programme of the meeting was based on Bible study. In the morning worship, expositions were given of ten 'key' biblical words. These formed the basis of Bible study in the four Sections into which the meeting divided. With this as background, the Sections discussed four themes of present importance for the understanding and practice of the Christian world mission: I. 'The Witness of Christians to Men of Other Faiths'; II. 'The Witness of Christians to Men in the Secular World'; III. 'The Witness of the Congregation in its Neighbourhood'; IV. 'The Witness of the Christian Church across National and Confessional Boundaries'. The meeting was also divided into five Committees, which reviewed the policy and programme of the Commission under the following heads: 1. Reference and Finance; 2. Education for Mission and Evangelism; 3. Laymen in World Mission; 4. Joint Action for Mission; 5. Structure and Relationships of the Commission.

The present volume contains the main records of the meeting. It includes the speeches given at it, and the outcome of its deliberations i n the reports of the Sections and a summary of the reports of the

Committees. It is hoped therefore that it conveys a fair and comprehensive impression of the meeting as a whole. Two points should, however, be noted in any use made of it. First, in view of the central place occupied by Bible study, reference should be made to the Biblical expositions published by the S.C.M. Press Ltd. under the title of *Key Words of the Gospel*, which also includes an abbreviated version of the opening sermon given by the Rev. Emilio Castro. Second, the present volume includes only a summary of the reports of the Committees. For the full text of these reports, together with a chronological record of the proceedings and other material, reference should be made to the *Minutes of the Second Meeting of the Commission on World Mission and Evangelism*, published by the Commission on World Mission and Evangelism, which constitutes the official record.

London   R. K. ORCHARD
March 1964

NOTES ON AUTHORS

Mr M. M. THOMAS is Director of the Christian Institute for the Study of Religion and Society in Bangalore, India.

The Rev. Dr W. A. VISSER 'T HOOFT is General Secretary of the World Council of Churches, Geneva.

The Rev. GONZALO CASTILLO-CÁRDENAS is Executive Secretary of the Committee on Presbyterian Co-operation in Latin America.

The Rev. AHARON SAPSEZIAN is General Secretary of the Association of Theological Seminaries in Brazil.

Pasteur JEAN KOTTO is Secretary General of the Evangelical Church of the Cameroun.

The Rev. ALFONSO LLOREDA is a Bible Translator for the Presbyterian Church in Mexico.

Canon JOHN V. TAYLOR is General Secretary of the Church Missionary Society, England.

The Rev. HARRY DANIEL is Presbyter of the Church of South India and leader of the Bangalore Industrial Service.

The Rev. GEORGE E. TODD is Director of the Department of Urban Church of the United Presbyterian Church in the U.S.A.

The Right Rev. Dr S. KULANDRAN is Bishop in Jaffna, Ceylon, in the Church of South India.

Professor Dr HEINRICH MEYER is Bishop of Lübeck and Professor of Missions at the University of Hamburg.

Pastor THOMAS EKOLLO is School Manager for the Evangelical Church of Cameroun.

The Rev. Dr c. h. hwang is Principal of Tainan Theological College, Formosa.

Dr robert w. spike is Secretary for Programme of the United Church Board for Homeland Ministries of the United Church of Christ, U.S.A.

Dr kathleen bliss is General Secretary of the Church of England Board of Education.

Prof. mauricio a. lópez is Secretary of the Department on Church and Society of the Division of Studies of the World Council of Churches.

THE WORLD
IN WHICH WE PREACH CHRIST

M. M. Thomas

THE 'aim' of the Commission on World Mission and Evangelism is 'to further the proclamation to the whole world of the Gospel of Jesus Christ, to the end that all men may believe in him and be saved'. There are two basic convictions here which are permanently present in the idea of the Christian mission. First, that God has sent Jesus Christ to be the Saviour of the world. Therefore all men everywhere need Jesus Christ and the salvation through faith in him. Secondly, the Church of Christ is called to communicate the Gospel of Jesus Christ to the whole world, so that all men may believe and be saved. If this communication is to be effective as communication it is important that we seek in each generation to know the world in which men live and to understand their basic thoughts, hopes, aspirations, and the urges within which they become aware of self and God. We must learn the patterns in which they hide from God and seek him, or enter into dialogue with him, in which he puts fundamental questions to them and they answer him 'Yes' or 'No'. For this reason while the mission is the same for all times and for all men, missions in which it finds expression must change from generation to generation and people to people. We may then consider some realities of the contemporary world which have revolutionized the patterns of man's understanding of nature, man and God, and of their search for salvation, which therefore compel rethinking or rather continued rethinking of Christian missions.

1. The Miraculous Expansion of 'Second Nature'

It is necessary to begin with the revolution which I know least from inside: the tremendous growth of science and technology in the recent past and the profound effects of man's new view of nature and

cosmos on his understanding of self, man and God. The debate on
Bishop Robinson's *Honest to God* has proved beyond doubt one fact,
namely that the images, myths and language of traditional religion
have become, or are increasingly becoming, irrelevant to men who
are growing up into the views and temper and lingua franca of the
modern scientific age. We are only at the beginning of this debate.
But apart from this question of world-view in which we speak of
God, we have to reckon with the fact that the scientific and technological revolution has brought about a real transformation in the character of nature and therefore in the relation of man to nature. In the
mountain province of the Philippines while attending an Asian tribal
consultation, I witnessed the pagan priests and people of Animism
sacrificing to mountain deities of fertility before the sowing of rice
seeds. With only subsistence technology in possession, hostile nature
conceived as peopled with supernatural deities has to be continuously
propitiated. I come from the plains of India, where religion has
moved far away from Animism, but it is still the most potent source
of popular religion, among not only the illiterate but also the educated.
This is shown by their constant dependence on raw nature—land, sun
and rain—for their livelihood, and by the constant fear of the influence
of stars. Science and technology certainly make a radical change at
this point. Man no more needs to depend on the hostility or the friend-
liness of first nature. He has mastered the powers of nature, and has
created out of it a 'second nature' which does his bidding. Three
implications need to be specially mentioned:

1. A heightened sense of human creativity. In one sense, the many
revolts against religion in the past two or three centuries have all been
to release man's creativity, which was suppressed by religion and the
dictates of religious authority. The relation of the Gospel to human
creativity is still to be thought out.

2. A heightened sense of mobility and dynamism. The Papal Encyc-
lical, *Pacem in Terris*, speaks of 'a pronounced dynamism' as characteristic of the contemporary world. Fixed structures are dissolving—
location, neighbourhood, work and status and even wife are shifting
constantly. As a result any idea of a law, given by God or the
moral order, is suspect. Man wants to assert the right to destroy old
structures of society and create new ones, and even to create himself
and his own ends. Evidently man has a new understanding of
creativity and we must acknowledge it in any consideration of

the relation between Creator and creature, law and love, grace and freedom.

3. With all the affirmation of man's mastery over nature and his ability to mould social structures through science and technology, there is a growing sense of powerlessness to consecrate the powers released by technology solely to human ends. Loneliness and self-alienation, and constant threat to the integrity of selfhood grow because in a highly technical society 'man has become mechanized, routinized and made comfortable as an object' and therefore 'in the profoundest sense displaced and thrown off balance as a subject'. What does the Gospel of reconciliation mean to this sense of alienation? The question shows a feature of the contemporary world, but the answer must be left, I think, to abler persons.

2. The Search for the Spiritual Dynamic of a New Pattern of Society

A second feature of the contemporary world is the revolutionary ferment created in Asia, Africa and Latin America by the more or less successful nationalist revolts against foreign domination and the present revolutionary programme of nation-building.

The most profound effect of it all has been at the level of man's search for the social conditions of his humanity within these continents. The terms of this search are very different at present from the search for the meaning of creativity, mobility and reconciliation in affluent and highly technical societies, where the problems of poverty and social justice have become more or less problems of the past. What then are some of the points at which the ferment inspired by nationalism and nation-building is revolutionizing the mind, heart and spirit of men as they seek a new human dignity and status?

People have long resigned themselves to poverty, considering it their fate. Today the revolt against poverty and the search for economic productivity have produced what has been called 'the revolution of rising expectations'.

People have long endured social inequality and oppression whether between man and woman, or between man and man, thinking that such inequality was divinely ordained justice. Today they are in revolt against it and seek to build a more equalitarian society. Social justice is a phrase charged with dynamism.

People have been content to live in conformity with customs and as functions of the traditional group, whether family, tribe, clan, caste or village. They did so because group-customs were sanctified by religion. Today men and women are conscious of the fundamental rights of individual personality and its freedom of nonconformity. The discovery of individual personality and its freedom in state, society and religion is a dynamic of radical social change in these areas.

Thus economic development, social justice and the fundamental rights of the human person are the goals of new societies which men in many nations set before themselves as they seek their dignity as men. But the more searching question relevant to our discussion here is: what are the cultural and spiritual foundations for this pattern of radical social change? Where will the dynamic of this social revolution come from? Not in the first place from traditional philosophies, cultures and religions; they have been too much a part of the old order, and need radical transformation to become an indigenous foundation for the new society. In fact, there is a search for a dynamic ideology which will buttress the new pattern of social humanism. Nationalism has come into being through the struggles for national freedom. But it needs to be related to a social ideology powerful enough to fight highly entrenched vested interests. And so we have the search for a social ideology which can speak of development, social justice and personal freedom not merely as ideals but with a sense of their relation to the ultimate nature and destiny of man and an ultimate interpretation of history. This is the situation in which the whole range of ideologies, different forms of liberalism, socialism and Marxism, have been battling for the soul of man. It is this situation which shapes the thinking of men regarding the meaning of life and human salvation among the people of these many countries.

The point I am making is that the search for a new pattern of human society and for an adequate spiritual dynamic for this pattern are realities of the contemporary world which are relevant to the task of defining missions today. Frankly, I do not think missions have given sufficient attention to defining the relation between salvation through faith in Christ and the search of men for a dynamic idea of man and history to nerve him in his political struggles for social renewal. Without this dimension, I must confess, I get sick of the debates on the relation between mission and service.

Incidentally the search for the ethos and dynamic of a genuine humanism is not only present *in* the several nations and societies, but it also grows as an important factor in the relations *between* the nations, peoples and cultures of the world. There is a growing sense of common humanity or human solidarity in the world which finds its expression in mutual concern, a sense of participation in the struggles of others for their fundamental rights, and a common endeavour in building structures of a world community and searching for an ethos to make them stable. This 'secular ecumenical movement' may be only beginning, but it is already a genuine movement of human solidarity which we must recognize as a new factor of no small significance in the world today. In fact, after Western expansion has been halted, the way in which the Western societies have responded to the call to participate in the struggle for new societies in the non-Western world is a most remarkable expression of this growing sense of common humanity.

When we think of ecumenical missions we cannot but ask the question: how are secular ecumenism and Christian ecumenism related to each other? What is the peculiar Christian witness of missions to and within secular ecumenism?

3. *The Religions of Mankind*

So far I have not dealt with the pattern of religious thought and life, because I wanted to show that the vital points at which God and man meet and enter into dialogue need not always be 'religious'. But the world of religions still remains the symbolic expression of man's apprehension of the ultimate meaning of life, the sphere within which idolatrous rebellions against God and his turning away from idols to serve the living God are both expressed in different religious acts of 'worship'. (I use the word here literally and not in its demythologized meaning.)

What are some of the tremendous changes taking place in the religions of mankind (including the Christian religion) and what are their significance to the Christian mission of salvation to the world today?

One thing can be said to be true, at least as a general world trend: the traditional institutional integration between religion, society and state is fast breaking down. The state, and to a lesser extent social institutions, are getting a large measure of autonomy to pursue their own ends free from the control of religion and religious authority.

The structures of Christendom broke down long ago, but even Protestant missions continued to conceive Christendom as an ideology, and in fact the mission compounds of Asia and Africa were set up as little Christendoms, as societies under Christian control. This was in part inevitable because non-Christian communities too were religious-doms and therefore a change of religion meant ostracism from traditional communities.

Such situations no doubt still exist. But with the granting of religious liberty as a fundamental right of the person by many nation-states today the general trend is definitely towards a break-up of this institutional integration of religion with political, economic and social institutions. To speak only of Asia, this growing separation of society and state from the control of traditional religions came about through the operation of many factors. To mention a few:

1. The necessity for a common basis of national unity and common efforts in nation-building in a situation of religious pluralism.
2. The struggle for fundamental rights and social justice against oppressive traditional social structures and customs. This involved opposition to religions also, as they were the main sanctions of the traditional social order.
3. The welfare state has taken the responsibility and control of large areas of life which until now were under religious control; it has legislated in matters which were till now under religious control and promoted community development based on neighbourhood rather than religion.
4. The increasing influence of a religiously neutral education in scientific knowledge and industrial technique.
5. The growth of industrial urban centres.

Through these forces secularization is coming to larger and larger areas of political and social life in all countries. Along with this process which brings a certain integrity to secular areas of life, secularism has also developed as a total philosophy and way of life. Often this has occurred without its becoming a dogma, although new secular dogmas of scientific rationalism, materialism and Marxism have emerged.

From what one reads one gets the impression that this secularization has gone furthest in the countries of Europe and the word 'religion-lessness' is used frequently to characterize European man. (I have some reservations at this point.) I suppose it means that as a separate activity religion has ceased to be a significant factor in the life of the bulk of the people. It also seems to mean that the ideas, beliefs, symbols and activities which are meant to express the meaning of life or the struggle for ultimate truth and love are not drawn from traditional religion and have no supernatural reference. This, however, would not be true, I presume, of several other areas of the world now, though the trend is in this direction.

There are two ways in which religions are finding new life. The first I would call a self-defensive reaction against secularization, secular ideologies and conversion to other religions. I do not know whether the presence of 'Christian' political parties in dominance in several countries of Western Europe means anything by way of expressing a nostalgia for the idea of Christendom in Europe. In Roman Catholic countries this is more evident. There is a great deal of defence of the white man's civilization. In Asian countries the militant political ideologies and parties of Hindu, Buddhist, Islamic and tribal religious nationalism are forceful in political life; they do exert dominant influence on the structure and policies of the state in some, more especially Islamic, countries. It is on the whole a backward-looking religious-cum-ethnic counterblast to social change itself.

The second is a creative renascence of ancient religions based on a reformation of religion. Leaders of renascent religions accept the secularization of large areas of social and political life as good for both religion and society, and what they seek to do is to provide a religious inspiration from within for the new autonomous areas of society and politics and a religious dynamic for man's struggle for radical social change. I am thinking of men like Vinobha Bhave in India.

In a sense we might say that renascent ancient religions are religions which are coming to adulthood by a recognition of the religious significance of secularism, the struggle for social humanism, and the seeking to provide them with a stable spiritual foundation. It is not altogether unlike the efforts of Christians in the same direction to provide a Christian basis for secularism and humanism.

One of the important results of the impact of modern realities on religions has been the recognition that religious truth should not be identified with any one culture. Religions should be considered as transcending all cultures and therefore capable of evaluating and transforming and taking new life in every culture. This is true of Christianity. It was only very recently that Christianity was identified uncritically with Western culture by the missions and the younger

Churches. It was nationalism that awakened Christians to the need and possibilities of indigenization of Christianity and brought liberation from this too easy identification of Christianity and Western culture, enabling the Churches to recover the essential universality of the Gospel. The strange thing that is happening today in all the ancient religions is that they too are ceasing to be ethnic cults wedded to a particular people or culture. They too are affirming their universal and missionary character, and their ability to find new homes in cultures other than those traditionally associated with them. Hindu and Buddhist missions have come to stay. Until very recently it was henotheism that Christian missions faced (that is, every culture with its own god). It is still present and that not only in tribal communities. Even Gandhiji opposed change of religion primarily on the basis that Hinduism was *Swadeshi* religion, the religion of India. But the dominant claim of Hinduism and Buddhism today is that they are universal religions. Their claim to universalism is parallel to the Christian claim to all-inclusiveness and ultimacy of Jesus Christ. During the recent centenary celebrations of Swami Vivekānanda, his words were quoted:

> Even Christians cannot understand their New Testament without understanding the Vedānta. The Vedānta is the rationale of all religions. Without the Vedānta every religion is superstition; with it everything becomes religion.

At this point it is clear we are in the realm of an either-or decision of faith.

Christianity, renascent religions and secular faiths, are all involved in the struggle of man for the true meaning of his personal and social existence—each in its own terms but together. It seems to me that the relation between Christian faith and other living religions and secular faiths is passing to a new stage, because they not only coexist in the same society but also co-operate to build a common secular society and culture. It is within such coexistence and co-operation that we can best enter into dialogue at the deepest level on the nature and destiny of man and on the nature of ultimate Truth. In this form the judgment and salvation of Christ himself can be proclaimed. Men, whether secular or religious, are asking questions today to which the Gospel is challengingly relevant. In his collection of essays, *Theology of Culture*, Paul Tillich says about Asian religions in the past:

The difficulty with the highly developed religions of Asia, for instance, is not so much that they reject the Christian answer *as answer*, as that their human nature is formed in such a way that they do not ask the questions to which the Gospel gives the answer. To them the Christian answer is no answer because they have not asked the question to which Christianity is supposed to give the answer. This is one example of the problem of participation.[1]

The significance of modern secularism and modern renascence of ancient religions is precisely that for the first time they are in a situation in which Christianity can participate because the questions which they are asking about human existence and salvation are those for which the Gospel has the answer. Men, whether secular or religious, are concerned with freedom, its responsibilities and anxieties, its purpose and tragedy so that questions about the meaning of existence including the problems of sin, law and grace, guilt and salvation, alienation and reconciliation, and the relation between justice and love are raised existentially. It is only as the Christian missions are patterned to participate in the common agony of articulating these questions and the answers to them within the framework of contemporary life and language, that they can understand in depth the meaning of Jesus Christ for today and communicate the Gospel of his salvation to others. As Paul Tillich says:

> True communication of the Gospel means making possible a definite decision for or against it.[2]

[1] Oxford University Press (New York, 1959), p. 204-5.
[2] Op. cit., p. 202.

MISSIONS
AS THE TEST OF FAITH

W. A. Visser 't Hooft

SØREN KIERKEGAARD has written that to live in this world means to be tested.[1] Life is a perpetual examination and God is the examiner. Even in Christ's life there is the testing of his obedience. But he is the only one whose life becomes the test of all other lives. When he ascends to heaven the great examination period for mankind begins and it lasts until his return. We are always thinking and talking about our achievements, but that is only making ourselves important. Whether we achieve something or not, is wholly God's affair. We have to be concerned only with this: whether we pass the examination and stand the test.

That is a radical attack on nearly all our various types of Christianity. Kierkegaard rejects at one and the same time the activist heresy and the intellectualist heresy. For he means to say that what counts in the examination is neither the sum of our activities nor the weight of our knowledge and understanding, but the nature of our commitment to God.

Kierkegaard has the Bible on his side. He does not even exaggerate by introducing the word examination. *Dokimazein*, testing, is indeed a technical term used by the Greeks for official examinations. But as so often the Bible pours new content into a current expression. The divine examination has its own specific characteristics. What these are we can find out by analysing those passages in the New Testament in which the testing of the faith is the central idea.

The *raison d'être* of the test is to establish faith in its genuine nature. Let faith be faith and nothing else. It is a pastoral and (with all respect to the teaching profession) not a professorial examination. It does not seek to ascertain how much spiritual, moral or intellectual baggage the student has been able to assemble, but whether he really counts on God and not on himself or on some other force. We read in 1 Peter 1:7, 'These trials come so that your faith may prove itself worthy of all praise, glory, and honour when Jesus Christ is revealed.' (N.E.B.)

[1] In *Einübung im Christentum*.

Roland de Pury wrote in the Gestapo prison in Lyons: 'It happens that God wants to have in his hand a little bit of really pure faith, a bit of love without anything else and that he then throws everything in the fire and lets Satan consume what is most precious to us.'[1]

The method of the examination is that of purification. Both 1 Corinthians 3 and 1 Peter 1 speak of the test by fire. All the impure elements which have attached themselves to the faith must be destroyed. According to Isaiah (1:25, R.S.V.) the Lord said to Israel: 'I will smelt away your dross as with lye and remove all your alloy.' The instruments of the examination are tribulations or troubles (literally pressures—*thlipsis*) and trials (*peirasmoi*) which are part and parcel of human existence in this world. Our Lord said: 'In the world you will have trouble' (Jn. 16:33, N.E.B.). In facing the pressures of the world we are simply sharing the life of Jesus himself. We are not to by-pass the Cross. But the troubles are not the last word. In the eschatological perspective they appear as a trial 'for a little while' (1 Pet. 1:6). The outcome of the examination is a faith that has stood the test. The English language has no word to translate *dokime* (in German *Bewährung*). That is why it comes to such a misleading translation as that of the Revised Standard Version of Romans 5:3 where *dokime* becomes 'character' so that the test of faith suddenly appears as a moral test. The New English Bible comes nearer to the original by translating: 'proof that we have stood the test'. This faith that has stood the test is closely bound up with the patient, but not passive, endurance, the *hypomone* which is equally characteristic of the Christian life. It can be said that the test produces the endurance (Jas. 1:3), but also that the endurance produces that quality of faith which has come victoriously through the test.

And the perspective in which the whole examination must be seen is that of hope and joy. Hope, for to pass the test is to be confirmed in the hope that one may share in the victory of Christ. And joy, because if through the trials we can still say: 'I have kept the faith', we know that Christ has also overcome the world in us.

The Missionary Witness as a Specific Test

What has this testing of the faith to do with missions? Faith is tested in various ways, but there is no more decisive test than the one

[1] *Pierres vivantes*, p. 21.

concerning the translation of faith into missionary witness. A central question in the great examination is: are you ready in all circumstances to proclaim that Christ is the Lord? It is with specific reference to the divine judgment that Jesus says: 'Whoever therefore shall confess me before men, him will I confess also before my Father which is in heaven. But whosoever shall deny me before men, him will I also deny before my Father which is in heaven.' (Mt. 10:32–3.) In Peter's life the first great test comes when he has to stand up to public opinion and fails to render witness. But he is graciously allowed to go up for a second examination and this time he not only knows the right answer, but gives it with boldness: 'We cannot but speak the things which we have seen and heard.' (Acts 4:20.) How closely the testing of the faith is linked up with its public proclamation becomes clear in the history of the word *martus*. The *martus* is at first simply the witness who gives testimony concerning facts, that is, in the New Testament context, the facts concerning the life and death and resurrection of Jesus of Nazareth. But this witness meets with strong opposition; it brings men into open conflict with the world. Their faith is tested: will they keep silent or even deny their Lord? Those who remain obedient have to suffer and some pay the price of death. The witness has become a martyr. He has passed the greatest examination of all and the examination had to do with his willingness to obey at all cost the calling to make the Gospel known to all men.

The Church has generally not much trouble in the world if it keeps its faith to itself. The conflict starts as soon as the Church goes out into the world and proclaims, as Paul did in Athens (Acts 17:30), that God 'commands mankind, all men everywhere, to repent' (N.E.B.). Justin describes the attitude of the world to the Church in these words: 'Go then all of you and kill yourselves, and pass even now to God, and do not trouble us.'[1] Paul Schneider is murdered in 1939 in Buchenwald not because he is a Christian, but because he is a witness, who insists on shouting the Gospel from his cell to his fellow-prisoners. It is the nature of the world that it does not want to be bothered by the Gospel.

There is another way in which the missionary and evangelistic witness is the test of faith. It is in that witness that the Church proves or disproves whether its faith is the real article, that is whether it is

---

[1] *The Second Apology of Justin*, trans. by M. Dods, G. Reith and B. P. Pratten, T. & T. Clark (1867), Chap. 4, p. 75.

wholly and exclusively rooted in the apostolic *kerygma*. It seems to me that this comes out most clearly in the following three questions:
1. It is in the missionary situation that the Church has to give a clear answer to the question: whether it believes in the 'happenedness' of the great deeds of God in Christ. The word 'happenedness' has, I believe, been introduced into the English language by von Hügel. He uses it to make the following decisively important point:

> Christianity . . . is not simply a doctrine of certain laws and principles of the spiritual life . . . the central conviction and doctrine of Christianity is the real prevenience and condescension of the real God . . . it is not a simple idea, but a solid fact; not something that so universally *ought* to happen, that in fact it never happens at all . . . Christianity cannot really do without this most humble seeming assurance of sheer happenedness . . .[1]

Now whether the Church believes fully in this happenedness will become manifest in its missionary witness. A Church which is not deeply penetrated by the faith that the crucial centre of all human history is what God has done, in and through Christ, will hardly undertake a sustained missionary effort and its witness will never have the toughness and resiliency, the patience and endurance without which missions cannot accomplish their task. It is only those who offer real news about divine deeds who will stand the test in the day of trouble.
2. In the second place it is in the missionary situation that the Church has to give a clear answer to the question whether it really believes in the universality of the Gospel. It is so easy to pay lip service to the truth that Christ is the Lord of mankind and that the one died for all men, but to live in fact as if Christ were a local saviour and the inventor of values for one of the many possible cultures or civilizations. By becoming missionary the Church confesses that Christ is the Saviour of all mankind. The report on the main theme of the Evanston Assembly says:

> . . . it is of special significance when the Gospel crosses geographical frontiers, for it is when a Church takes the Gospel to another people and another land that it bears its witness to the fact that the new age has dawned for all the world.[2]

[1] F. von Hügel, *Essays and Addresses on the Philosophy of Religion*, Second Series, Dent (1926), p. 107-8 (U.S. edition, E. P. Dutton & Co. Inc.).
[2] Report of the Advisory Commission on the Main Theme of the Second Assembly of the World Council of Churches, Harper Bros. (1954), p. 18.

3. In the third place it is in the missionary situation that the Church has to give a clear answer to the question whether it really believes that the Word of God is not bound. A Church may have great missionary fervour and yet fail to be truly apostolic, because its missionary work consists in the exporting of its own culturally conditioned brand of Christianity and in the imposing of that brand on another people. If so, it has not grasped that the Word of God cannot and must not be imprisoned in any human form of expression but claims the sovereign right to make its own impact upon every people and to create its own forms of expression.

Missions Tested by the Modern World

The missionary witness is at all times a test of the faith of the Church. But there are times when the testing process is more or less hidden (we might speak of underground testing). And there are other times when the testing is very much above ground and demonstrably acute. The normal situation is rather the situation of open conflict. Must we not look on the period from roughly the middle of the nineteenth to the middle of the twentieth century as a sort of armistice-period in the relation betwen missions and the world? The contradiction of the world was more or less *sotto voce* and there was sufficient outside encouragement so as not to notice these negative voices. The encouragement which came from the world and sometimes even from the Church was often given for the wrong reasons. Somehow missions seemed to become an accepted part of modern civilization.

It would seem that we are now entering into a different period again. Tambaram—just twenty-five years ago—had already a first glimpse of this change. May I quote myself? My main impression of Tambaram was expressed in these words:

> The Church is in the process of becoming truly universal and precisely at the moment when that universality becomes evident, it enters into a crucial conflict with the forces which dominate the world.[1]

At that time we thought of course especially of the various totalitarianisms. In the last twenty-five years that conflict has become more acute. Many more Churches have become churches under pressure. The

[1] International Christian Press and Information Service, January 1939, NO. 4.

numbers of non-Christians living outside the reach of any form of organized evangelistic and missionary action have vastly increased. And the so-called Christian countries are more and more becoming 'pays de mission'. Other great world religions have become mission-minded and enter, not without success, the traditionally Christian territories. At the same time the right of the Church to be a missionary church is challenged in all parts of the world.

The opponents of missions come from the most differing quarters and must sometimes feel bien étonnés de se trouver ensemble. There are the totalitarian ideologists who pretend that they want to fight a clean ideological fight against all attempts of the Christian Church to infect the minds of people, particularly of the young, with the anti-social Christian message. But they are really afraid of a purely ideological battle and so they use the weapons of administrative pressure. It is incomprehensible to them that, in spite of all, the Churches in their domain still continue to live and sometimes to grow. Then there are the syncretists, the increasingly successful groups and sects in all parts of the world which advocate a total integration of all the religions, and the philosophical syncretists who work out new all-inclusive religions on paper. Prof. Northrop of Yale desires:

> ... that Western religious leaders with an adequate idea of the good and the divine will go to the East more to acquire its religion of intuition and contemplation than to convert the Easterner to the Western theistic religion of doctrine and reform.[1]

Such voices have become legion in all our countries and these ideas are now penetrating with great rapidity into wider circles, including Christian circles. Next there are the internationalists who are concerned with the peaceful coexistence of all civilizations and who believe that missions are basically a form of cultural invasion and therefore an obstacle to the creation of the right international relationships. Again we have the cultural nationalists who are the modern defenders of the old principle cuius regio, eius religio. They see religion as part of the cultural heritage which they want to defend at all costs. And there are the advocates of an universal tolerance, many of them men and women of the finest calibre who consider the missionary spirit as a spirit of arrogance. Simone Weil whose life we cannot fail to admire writes:

[1] F. S. C. Northrop, The Meeting of East and West, Macmillan Co. (1946), p. 455.

Personally, I should never give even as much as a sixpence towards any missionary enterprise. I think that for any man a change of religion is as dangerous a thing as a change of language is for a writer. It may turn out a success, but it can also have disastrous consequences.[1]

Vestdijk, the leading author in Holland, says that a Christianity which is not willing to give up the claim that it alone has validity is likely to make itself 'hopelessly ridiculous in the eyes of the Asians'.[2] And so we could go on and cite Arnold Toynbee or Carl Gustav Jung, Radhakrishnan or Aldous Huxley and a host of others. We may finally add that the image of the missionary in the modern novel is generally that of an incredibly narrow-minded person who has not the slightest understanding of the people and culture to which he has been sent.

The consensus of the *Zeitgeist* is clear. It is an anti-missionary consensus. And nearly all the signs in the realm of politics and of ideas point in the direction of increasing rather than decreasing unwillingness to recognize the *raison d'être* of missions. A new testing time for missions has arrived.

The Missionary Attitude in a Testing Time

How shall we react? The first thing to say is that we should not be surprised at this development and should therefore not complain. The world is simply doing its wordly job. The world is quite right from its point of view. Missions *is* an impossible undertaking from every point of view except the one of the faithful Church which cannot hold its tongue about the world-shaking revelation which it has received. St John says: 'Do not wonder, brethren, that the world hates you,' (1 Jn. 3:13, R.S.V.), and St Peter: 'do not be surprised at the fiery ordeal which comes upon you to prove you, as though something strange were happening to you' (1 Pet. 4:12, R.S.V.). Well, we have not so much to do with hate and with an ordeal but with total incomprehension of our real calling. So we have even less reason for surprise.

Let the world be the world, but then let the Church be the Church. If we live once again in a time when we are under pressure this is

[1] *Letter to a Priest*, Routledge & Kegan Paul (1953), p. 33.
[2] *De toekomst der religie*, Van Loghum Slaterus (1947), p. 308.

deeply meaningful. It means that we are called to take the royal road indicated in Romans 5. The troubles are to lead us first to *hypomone*, endurance. Not merely a quietistic acceptance of the situation, but rather an active identification with the Lord, with his strange Gospel and his scandalous Cross. That implies, of course, that we do not dream of giving up one bit of the fundamental *kerygma*. On the contrary. Now that the world has become sharply critical and seeks to silence us, we have a new opportunity to make it very clear that we really mean what we say and that our only motive is that the world may believe that in Jesus Christ God reconciled the whole world to himself. In the Book of Revelation these three belong together: the suffering and the kingship and the endurance (Rev. 1:9). These three are ours in Jesus. The King helps us to endure. And our endurance consists in proclaiming that he is the King of Kings.

The next station on the road of Romans 5 is the faith which has stood the test, that is, the faith which has been purified. Tested missions are missions which have cleaned up their house. They listen therefore to their critics. For is it not possible that the Great Examiner uses these critics for his purposes? Must we not learn from the wild attacks of the Communists that we have obscured the prophetic message of social justice; from the criticism of the internationalists that we have given an individualistic rather than a truly cosmic and universal interpretation of Christianity; from the ironical comments of the advocates of tolerance that we have often been arrogant, rather than humble, in our proclamation of the Lord whom we have not chosen, but has chosen us?

Missions which are undergoing the divine test cannot afford to add any additional, non-essential scandal to the great inevitable scandal of the Cross. They become so ashamed of the scandal of a divided witness and a divided Church that they hasten to undo the damage which they have done by their disunity and seek to go as far as humanly possible in their common planning and their joint action for mission. They seek to efface any traces of foreignness which obscure the witness and make it easy for the world to dismiss missions as cultural invasions from another continent. They seek especially to avoid even the slightest appearance that they have any interest in maintaining control over the Churches which they have helped to found. Tested missions defend nothing else than the right to bring the Gospel to all men. And in defending that right they are aware that it must not be defended by means of power but by the inherent force of the witness itself.

There is on our road a final station. The faith that is tested produces hope. It is one of the strangest aspects of the history of the Church that the Churches under pressure often know so much more about hope than the untroubled Churches. There is the joy of experiencing that, in spite of the difficulty of the examination and one's obvious incapacity to respond adequately, one is somehow allowed to pass. There is the joy that, in spite of all the closing of doors, the Word of God still finds holes through which it can creep. And there is above all the glad discovery that we are taken up in the great happenedness which goes on happening and will lead to the ultimate event of the manifest victory of Christ.

If it is at the point of its missionary witness that the Church is specially tested, it is also at that point that it is given ground for hope.

a. The Life and Witness
of the Church in Latin America

THE LIFE AND WITNESS
OF THE CHURCH IN LATIN AMERICA

Gonzalo Castillo-Cárdenas

THERE are many different factors that lift into prominence the historical importance of this meeting. The very fact that it is being held in Latin America is an additional factor of great significance to us in this continent. A great deal of water has gone under the bridge since Edinburgh. If the assembly in 1910 negated the idea of Protestant missions in Latin America, we would like to understand this meeting as supporting that idea, as it were an outstretched hand that says to us, 'We are with you now in your missionary task.' We have followed with interest and elation the gradual change of attitude, the modification and transition that has culminated now in this meeting in Mexico.

The Protestant Presence in Latin America

No one today would doubt the legitimacy of the Protestant presence in Latin America, mainly because no one holds any longer to the naïve illusion of a 'Catholic continent'. This is now considered a myth by technical studies of the matter.[1] The present revolutionary changes that now grip the continent have brusquely 'demythologized' the concept of a religious continent, bringing to light its dechristianization and secularism. A distinguished priest of Uruguay, Father R. Segundo, has put it this way:

> . . . the basic process of dechristianization is going on in all the large cities of Latin America. At one time social pressure could

[1] Note, for example, the article by Father François Malley, in *Informations Catholiques Internationales*, September 15th, 1962.

be regarded an assistant in the work of Christianization; it was a kind of 'machine to make Christians' . . . as soon as this machine stopped functioning there seemed nothing left of the old traditions of Catholic countries. In Latin America the time is fast approaching when there will no longer be Christians except through evangelization. But to our great amazement we are beginning to realize that we do not know how to evangelize any longer.[1]

In the providence of God, Protestant Christianity arrived in Latin America at a time when this hard fact which Father Segundo describes began to be more evident. And it arrived possessed of a contagious passion, that of evangelism, and of a powerful instrument to realize that end, the Bible. These two elements of the evangelical presence irresistibly attracted the unevangelized masses, on one side, and on the other side attracted a whole array of 'reverse Christians' (as someone has called them: those who call themselves Catholics, baptizing their children and marrying in the Roman Church, but who are militantly opposed to all that is central in Catholicism—Pope, hierarchy, saints, church, confession, etc.). This explains the galloping expansion of Protestant Christianity in Latin America. In fact the majority of observers speak of 'dramatic' and 'phenomenal' growth. According to a study which has just appeared[2] the Protestant membership has multiplied 340 times in the last forty-five years; in the same period the number of organized local churches has increased 320 fold. Today, according to the same study, the total number of Protestants has reached nine million, which is five per cent of the total population of the continent.

Iberian Catholic Influences in the Latin American Protestant Movement

How can we characterize a phenomenon so exuberant and multiform, so unco-ordinated and dispersed, as is the Latin American Protestant movement? One way to do this is to describe it in relation to its Roman Catholic context.

It is a fact that Latin American Protestantism has inevitably assumed

---

[1] 'The Future of Christianity in Latin America', *Cross Currents*, Vol. XIII, No. 3, Summer 1963, pp. 276–7 and 280.
[2] *A Factual Study of Latin America*, by W. Stanley Rycroft and Myrtle M. Clemmer, United Presbyterian Church in the U.S.A. (1963).

a permanent posture of contradiction, rectification, and alternative to Iberian Catholicism, and that this posture has profoundly conditioned its own form of thought and emphases, as well as its negations and oppositions. Out of this tension are derived both the vigour and validity of the Protestant presence and also its limitations and liabilities.

As to the former, its vigour and validity, the Protestant movement has in place of religious superficiality emphasized the necessity of a deep spiritual communion with Christ; against syncretism it has upheld the supreme centrality of Jesus Christ in the Church and in personal and corporate piety; to the divorce between the moral and the religious, it has stressed the absolute necessity of a new birth with visible fruits in private life; to ignorance of the Scriptures, it has made the reading and the study of the Bible a requirement for membership in the Christian community; in place of a religiously passive laity, it has stressed the responsibility and participation of every believer in both the government of the Church and its evangelistic outreach. These have been and continue to be the great distinctives which give validity and power to the Protestant movement in Latin America.

On the other hand the exaggeration or corruption of certain truths by Iberian Catholicism has produced the effect of a clouding of the minds of the Protestants which has in turn prevented them from discovering and appreciating the truth underlying historic forms that are partially in error. This explains the existence of several serious limitations in the Protestant Churches of this continent, such as their difficulty in appreciating the transcendent reality of the Church, their failure to recognize the importance of visible unity, and their tendency to neglect the social and political implications of the Christian mission. To this day, in great segments of Latin American Protestantism, every attempt to recognize the importance of these aspects of the nature and mission of the Church is neutralized by a panic-fear of falling into 'Catholic errors'.

The Crisis Today

All of this, however, corresponds to the infancy and childhood of the Protestant movement, to its formative stage. Today there exists a new situation which is taking all of the Churches by surprise. The Protestant-Catholic alternative, although valid, has been pushed into the background of the scene by the tremendous pressures of social and political problems. In this new situation both Catholicism and Protestantism find themselves unable to evangelize the Latin American man. In the case of Protestantism, this is all the more pronounced among the older denominations. In spite of certain reports of advance in evangelism, the facts indicate that we have arrived at a point of stagnation and crisis. The Churches are making tremendous efforts merely to preserve what they have accomplished, but this labour of preservation and consolidation is made difficult because the youth decline to collaborate with their elders in a work which appears to them to be innocuous. The new generation of Protestants does not seem to find in the Churches the human and Christian sensitivity which the situation demands and they have turned apathetic or even opposed to the Church.

This 'internal' problem of the Church is a reflection of the total situation in Latin America, the main element of which is, in my opinion, the awakening of the collective conscience to the fact that we live in a society unjustly organized, which does not justify the sacrifice of the millions of human beings which is being required for its preservation. Thus the masses are determined to sacrifice their lives—not in order to preserve an unjust social order—but rather to change it radically. In this climate of high tension the mere doctrinal orthodoxy, personal piety, the rites and solemn assemblies according to one or another conception of God, and in general the traditional forms of life and the 'programmes' of the Churches—all this has become for the masses not merely irrelevant, but an offence to God and man unless those who profess to believe accept the human situation of the people as a primary responsibility and offer their lives to change it. This total situation confronts the Churches with challenging questions and demands which are themselves a whole array of additional problems.

One group of these problems derives from the new nationalism which the situation is creating. This is a healthy nationalism which is the struggle of the people to find themselves. Latin America is a continent in search of its own soul, and in order to gain this self-discovery it is necessary to tear away all of the underbrush that is suffocating the tender plant of its personality. This nationalism proposes certain legitimate questions to the Protestant Churches, requiring them to submit to a process of *kenosis* and incarnation in the new situation in Latin America. This requirement appears all the more justifiable because, with the exception of certain autochthonous groups of Pentecostals, the missionary agencies have brought too much foreign baggage. For the Church's mission today the problem is not the foreignness of this baggage but the fact that it places an additional burden on the Churches in the fulfilment of their missionary task in the new situation. This, in part, explains the difficulties with evangelism at the moment.

Another aspect of the same problem has to do with the personnel and financial aid that comes from abroad for the missionary work. When the major portion of these resources are provided by the same country—one which is in other aspects labelled imperialist—it is inevitable that the Church is exposed to the questions and suspicions of a people that is daily gaining greater self-awareness. Does not this amount, they ask, to another capitalist 'investment', this time of religious character? This question, which comes from outside the Church, would want importance were it not that many Latin American Churches in actual fact function as 'branches' of foreign organizations. What are the steps to be taken in order to destroy these barriers that make evangelism more difficult and in order to give more ample expression to the unity and the universality of the Church? This is a question of great importance for the evangelistic task of Protestant Churches in Latin America.

Another series of problems has to do with Protestant division. It is inevitable that peoples that desperately seek links of unity, of solidarity, of mutual loyalty for the great work of national development, look uneasily and even with distrust on the multiplicity of Protestant groups. Won't Protestantism, they ask, be an additional factor of national disintegration? This is a justified fear that raises one more barrier to the missionary task. In regard to Christian unity the problem is that the majority of Protestants in Latin America prefer a spiritual, romantic or abstract concept of unity, out of the fear that, were unity to be expressed in a visible and organic form, it would tend to suffocate personal liberty and lead the Church into a search for political power, into Iberian Catholic errors, whose consequences we as Protestants have suffered in Latin America. On the other hand, certain foreign mission organizations seem to be determined to prevent every move the 'national' believers try to make toward the healing of these divisions. These factors explain why the larger part of Protestants have barely begun to be aware of the theological contradiction of division and its disastrous consequences for evangelism. It is necessary, however, to give time for the great ecumenical preoccupations to stir and disturb the Latin American conscience *from within*. To try to transplant these concerns *from the outside* would be to commit the same error as that of importing the divisions in the first place. And the outcome the second time would be worse than the first. Thus when Christians from other continents concern themselves with Christian unity in Latin America it is necessary for them to exercise an extra amount of that Christian virtue which is already so desperately needed, namely patience.

Demolition and Reconstruction

Finally I would like to underline those social and political factors which are for Protestant believers exacting the most agonizing decisions. No one is ignorant of the fact that the Latin American people are faced with a double task, on the one hand that of demolition of an evil social and political order, whose beneficiaries are trying to preserve it at all costs, and on the other hand the gigantic task of construction of a new society for which a blue-print does not yet exist and which must be drawn up under the pressures of history and popular will. Today this demolition and construction have become more urgent because people no longer accept poverty, illiteracy and social injustice as an inevitable condition, but cherish the faith that it is possible to build a new social edifice capable of being a home worthy of the Latin American people. This very belief actually constitutes a marvellous conversion from fatalism to hope, from indolence to revolutionary action, from resignation to rebellion.

In the middle of this revolution-in-process the Christian suffers as he is beseiged by agonizing decisions. Should he isolate himself, take refuge in personal piety, flee contamination in search of his own salvation? Or had he better intervene in the situation in order to help avoid an abrupt change, seeking to preserve the established order with the hope of being able—gradually—to purify, improve and humanize it? Or should he perhaps give himself over heart and soul to a revolutionary programme proving his loyalty to the Gospel by his identification with this programme or party?

These questions are inextricably bound up with the Church's work of evangelization, with its Christian service, with its corporate life, that is, with its total mission. But the Churches find themselves desperately short of the theological and biblical reflection, the social ethics, with which to respond coherently to the agonizing questions of their members, especially their youth, whereas Marxism seems to offer concrete answers and specific remedies to the burning problems of the moment. Right within the Church there is perplexity, confusion, disorientation. Many Christians, whose consciences have been sensitized by the preaching of the Gospel—among them some seminary students—have chosen to abandon the Church and become Communist leaders. Others find that their loyalty to the Word of God requires them to participate *as Christians*, both in the demolition and in the construction, running all the risks and living with all the ambiguities of the revolution. In doing this they have suffered rejection by their elders and frequently by the hierarchy of their Churches. The Protestant Christian in Latin America now lives with this agony. It is the price of living 'in the midst of the times', where the voice of the Lord is heard: 'See, I have set you . . . to pluck up and to break down, . . . to build and to plant . . . For I am with you, says the Lord . . .' (Jer. 1:10, 19, R.S.V.). But, how shall we obey the Lord concretely in these days?

For the Protestant movement in Latin America the present crisis does not mean, in any sense, defeat. It is rather the time when great decisions are to be made. And the Churches are taking this tremendous problem to God in prayer, seeking his will through the study of both the Bible and the present-day situation in Latin America. Two years ago there was held in Huampaní, Peru, the first Latin American Evangelical Consultation on Church and Society. Its analysis of the problem has helped many Protestant Christians in their decisions. Ever since 1955 the Evangelical Confederation of Brazil has sponsored, through its Section on the Social Responsibility of the Church, study conferences on various aspects of the crisis to which we have referred. The most recent conference in this series (Recife, Brazil, July 1962), took as its theme, 'Christ and the Revolutionary Process in Brazil'. Last week (December 1st to 8th) in Bogotá, Colombia, there was a study congress of the Presbyterian and Reformed Churches in Latin America working under the theme 'The Nature and Mission of the Church Today', in which an effort was made to understand and respond to the principal challenges that confront the Churches today. All of this means that Protestant Christianity in this continent is at work preparing itself to act responsibly in the crisis that has arisen. In doing this the Churches are discovering with new freshness and power the relevance of the Gospel for all of the life of their peoples, deepening their conviction that the Christian faith is not merely equal to the magnitude of the gravest crisis, but is in fact greater than all crises.

THE LIFE AND MISSION
OF THE CHURCH IN BRAZIL

Aharon Sapsezian

THE pressure of the facts of life in the modern world on the one hand, and the more profound understanding of certain biblical perspectives on the other, have forced our generation of Christians to come to grips in a more concrete and real way with the Church in its totality, compelled by its total mission to the total world. The renewal of the Church in its exact sense as understood in and proceeding from the current ecumenical movement, consists precisely in the rediscovery of the biblical, Christological and universal character of the Church, and of the mission of this Church towards man in his total, historical and concrete being. This move towards renewal is the general characteristic of the Church in our time and as such it has its repercussions, in diverse ways, in the life of the Church of Jesus Christ in Brazil.

Even in a paper like this one, drastically limited in its compass and written from a distinctive Protestant perspective, this vision of the wholeness of the Church and its mission cannot be lost. And this vision must be maintained not just because it is by the courtesy of the World Council of Churches that we are meeting here to discuss these matters. There are at least two initial reasons why these concepts of renewal and of the wholeness of the Church are incorporated throughout the brief remarks which will follow. In the first place, Brazil is a country of almost continental proportions, currently in the midst of a dynamic search for its own national integration and identity. It is a nation that is working with firm determination to create a more fruitful and just social order, which means to break with the anachronisms and errors of the past. In such a situation any church that is more than a mere spectator of history will feel itself called to transcend any and all partial loyalties and relative values that hamper the execution of its historical mission or compromise its witness before men. Indeed, the Church can do no other because it is called upon to be loyal and obedient to Christ, who is the Lord of the whole Church, and of all *history. And it is becoming more and more difficult for the Church in Brazil to remain on the margin of history.

The second reason that imposes on us the necessity of adopting the perspective of the whole Church is that modern Brazil offers a panorama of Christian pluralism, of Christianity in all its usual forms, that makes it impossible for any church to escape the encounter with the 'other Church'. This encounter comes today sometimes in the form of apologetics, all too reminiscent of a well known polemic era in the life of our Churches; but more frequently today the encounter takes the form of dialogue. In a country of traditional Roman Catholic influence and preponderance—although let it be noted that this influence and preponderance has not always succeeded in expressing itself effectively—the Reformed version of the Church made extraordinary progress which has won for it the not always flattering or even always still true title of 'the fastest growing Church in the world'. This progress destroyed the myth that the Brazilian people are inherently Roman Catholic and gave legitimacy to the Protestant mission in Brazil, while at the same time it contributed decisively to assuring religious liberty to the other Christian and non-Christian religious groups that help form the Brazilian religious picture.

At this juncture we would like to start by making some brief observations concerning the most recent arrival on the pluralistic Brazilian Christian scene, that is, the Orthodox Church, although we admit the reference to this Church may surprise some who are not aware of its existence in our country. Brazil is a country of immigrants, and as such it has been receiving, especially since World War II, large contingents of Orthodox Christians from the countries of Eastern Europe and the Near East, belonging to the Russian, Greek and Syrian Patriarchates or others. Though still confined to communities of national origin, the Orthodox Christians already constitute a significant group of about 200,000 people in Brazil (larger than several traditional Protestant groups), and they are beginning to give some new forms and make their distinctive contributions to the Brazilian ecclesiastical scene. They represent a different form of the Christian faith to the eyes of many Brazilians, and they could have a significant effect upon the understanding and enrichment of certain aspects of the nature and life of the Church. This will depend, naturally, upon the manner in which these groups find their way to integrating and relating themselves within the life of the nation in its current dynamic phase. It will depend on the way they will take and accept the natural and inexorable process of being assimilated as their members involve themselves in the destiny of their new homeland.

In the immediate future the vocation of these Orthodox Churches seems to be to preserve the basic framework of the Christian heritage of their members, moderating the impact of a totally different culture that tends to be highly disintegrating in its effect on such communities, and tends even to alienate its members from their national Churches, which are the only source of Christian community in such cases. The manifestation of Christian solidarity on the part of the Brazilian Churches towards their Orthodox brethren seems today to consist principally in the difficult but necessary service of aid and orientation to the immigrant, which is a first expression of Christian love to the recently arrived.

To talk in this way about Christian pluralism in Brazil ought not to obscure the fact that the great majority of the Christian population continues firmly, even if not very conscientiously, linked to the Roman Catholic Church. The facts of this adherence have been studied both by Catholics and opponents, in works sometimes complacent and sometimes critical. It is not easy to draw an exact and simple profile of this Church, and this is true of Roman Catholicism in general, and much more so of this Church in the changing Brazilian scene. In spite of considerable changes in this Church during the different stages of Brazilian history, it will not be unfair to say however that it still maintains its original Iberian character, with its accentuated type of clericalism and being in large measure somewhat sluggish in adjusting to the new situations that are developing. But this general statement must be qualified by the undeniable fact that, as in other countries, Roman Catholicism in Brazil is living through a phase of awakening and the development of a new conscience. The most evident sign of this fact is the effort that the Roman Church is making to know itself better and more objectively, taking seriously its own weaknesses and exercising, in a new and courageous way, internal self-criticism.

We would like to enumerate some examples of this self-analysis of the Roman Church in Brazil at this moment: first, an intensification and renewal of the missionary task by taking seriously certain sections of Brazilian society that are no longer reached by the usual catechetical, devotional and liturgical forms, as for example workers, students and intellectuals; second, a greater identification with groups and social movements that are aspiring to a reform of the archaic structures of Brazilian political, social and economic life, structures that are responsible for much of the unnecessary poverty of many, especially in the rural areas; third, a search for means to disentangle the Christian faith from the syncretistic and superstitious influences that impregnate the popular religiosity of a considerable portion of Brazilian Roman Catholics; and fourth, the gradual and conscientious abandonment of the traditional attitude of hostility and repression toward the Protestant and other religious minorities.

Admitting that it is till too early to draw any definite conclusion as to the results of these renewing tendencies, we can, nevertheless, at least recognize the value of the intentions of those who promote them and, to say the least, be hopeful. It is the task of the Brazilian Protestant Church, above all, to follow attentively these movements of awakening and reform, because it is the Protestant Church, due to a natural reaction to certain historical facts in the past, that has developed in this country a form of attenuated but, I should say, chronic anti-Catholicism that often impedes it from seeing objectively some positive and fresh elements in Roman Catholicism. More than is generally thought or admitted, the Protestant Churches in Brazil have been moulded in their style of life and have planned their strategy of mission and evangelism in response to and in reaction to the pervasive Roman Catholic presence and mentality. Consequently, any serious change that occurs in Brazilian Catholicism will not fail to affect the action and, perhaps, the life of Protestant Churches which, after all, are constituted even today mainly by people who have come from peripheral Catholicism.

We turn now to Protestantism in Brazil. In order to characterize it, we fall back on categories that have become, even more so today, indispensable for the understanding of this Church. These categories are 'young Protestantism' on the one hand, and 'adult Protestantism' on the other. They were used by one of the most discerning scholars of Brazilian Protestantism, Emile Léonard, some fifteen years ago. Léonard characterized 'young Protestantism' by its 'zeal for evangelism and appropriate ecclesiastical organization', while 'adult Protestantism' is seen as concerned with the 'study of deficiencies of its ecclesiastical machinery and with doctrinal problems'. These terms and definitions are, of course, used with reference to Brazilian Protestantism.[1]

From the viewpoint of visible manifestations it can be said that it is 'young Protestantism' that first impresses the observer of the Protestant panorama in Brazil, and it is this group among Protestant groups, that appears to have the greatest impact among the great mass of Brazilians. Numerically speaking it is also the largest portion of the Protestant population in Brazil. Its most outstanding characteristic is, without doubt, the extraordinary aggressiveness in evangelism; indifferent to ecclesiastical formalities and sometimes even to doctrinal substance, it reaches with a moving and appealing message many in the most typical sector of the Brazilian population: the mass of urban and rural workers who are found in the lower economic and cultural social groups. Of this Church it can be truthfully said that it grows. I remember one of its pastors who told me that in six years of pastoral work he had started six new churches and that his goal was to start a new church each year of his career in the ministry. It is noted also for the immediacy or even urgency of its message, although it may be considered devoid of any sophistication. During Holy Week I heard a pastor of the 'Congregação Cristão', one of the branches of the group we are considering, speak of the power of the Resurrected Christ to overcome the evil eye, the voodoo spells and other forms of black magic that frightened many of his hearers who evidently had come from superstition, primitive spiritism or pseudo-Catholicism. But perhaps the greatest power of these churches is to be found precisely in their aptitude for giving their followers a meaningful communal life, a 'sense of belonging'. These churches make their greatest gains among those who have been uprooted and displaced by social and economic forces, and these congregations give to many of these people, men and women, white, brown and Negroes, a solidarity in life with others who have similar anxieties and hopes, in which they feel wanted and indeed are sought out to become part of a close group with a sense of mission.

This 'young Protestantism' with its almost euphoric vitality is not limited to the groups conventionally called 'Pentecostal'. In greater or smaller degree, it appears also in the historic Protestant Churches in Brazil. It is frequently the case that pastors who, discouraged with

[1] See E. Léonard, *O Protestantismo Brasileiro*, Associação de Seminários Teológicos Evangélicos (1963), p. 314.

the apparent rigidity of their traditional churches which seems impractical and unfruitful, deliver themselves to this type of aggressive enthusiasm that gives them a certain feeling of relevancy and often liberates them from frustrations which, no doubt, demand more radical and serious solutions.

There are two problems, among others, that this 'young Protestantism' is beginning to confront, and whose seriousness seems to be increasing day by day. First, the 'salvationist' Gospel that continues to emphasize redemption 'from the world', ought to be made whole by stressing also redemption 'in the world' and 'for the world'. Its primarily moralistic and individualistic ethic needs to be further developed in the sense of a more biblical concept of the social nature of Christian responsibility. It is lamentable that these groups which represent such a considerable number of the most typical portion of the Brazilian people, and who in their daily lives find themselves in the vortex of the contemporary dynamic historical process (of which they are often victims), when they are 'converted' deprive themselves of any responsible and significant participation 'in the world'. The most recent attempts at organizing for political purposes among these groups seem to be motivated more by a sense of potential political prestige, electoral leverage and power rather than as the result of any reflection about the vocation of a Christian in secular and political life.

The second problem 'young' Protestant groups face, which proceeds from their normal evolution, is that as they tend to become 'adult' churches, they must either make certain cultural, organizational and ethical adjustments, or they will run the risk of becoming merely a church of first-generation converts, with a strong evangelistic impact, but weak in the work of building up believers. In other words, unless these churches find a new depth to their life and being, they will often lose as many second-generation Christians out the back door as they receive new converts through the front door.

We would like here to reaffirm that it is essentially important to take seriously and to observe without prejudice what we have been calling the 'young' Protestant Church. It is not a second-class, or marginal Protestantism. In spite of its undeniable differences from the other, 'adult', Protestantism, it ought to be viewed with interest and hope. Perhaps it will be necessary to develop specific new categories to do justice to this Church and to understand its relation to the whole Church. As a matter of fact, whatever else these churches may represent they represent a searching criticism of the conventional life of the older Churches, and they manifest one way of responding to the serious problem—to which the whole Church is seeking the answer—of how to talk intelligibly of Christ to the growing mass of the Brazilian population, above all to the humble, the illiterate, the under-privileged, the neglected.

Our attention must be turned now to the 'adult Protestantism' in Brazil. When we remind ourselves that this Church has, as a general rule, only about a hundred years of history, it is easy to see that the phrase has only relative value and that its meaning is limited to the Brazilian situation. Of foreign origin, this Protestantism has rooted itself firmly, though not yet totally, in Brazilian soil. There is today, in the full sense of the phrase, a Brazilian Protestantism, established in practically every section of the country, recognized and respected by Roman Catholics, by Government authorities and by the people in general.

It is very useful to look again at some of the reasons that have caused this Church to be put in the place of honour that it occupies today. It may be argued that these reasons now belong to past history, but they will always have some suggestive value for present-day situations.

First, historic Protestantism in Brazil knew how to exploit the anti-clerical and anti-Roman sentiments among the more educated class in the closing years of the last century. The presentation of a Gospel that was ethical without being authoritarian, romantic without being mystical, and rational without being speculative, brought significant results in a *milieu* where the ideas of Comte's positivism has impregnated the cultured sections of the population. Second, intense educational work which complemented and was itself a means of evangelism counted much for the acceptance of Protestantism. The Protestant schools, very much pioneers in this country in introducing and using modern educational methods, were a real and valuable service to a nation eager for education, and a significant way of being present in the world and in the life of the nation. Third, Protestantism came on the Brazilian scene with the dynamizing and renewing impact over the traditional religion of the people through the proclamation of a Christ who demanded radical and audacious decisions. Though the work of the Protestants was considered proselytism by some (and indeed Protestantism of the era of polemics justified proselytism by insisting that the Roman Catholic Church was not a Christian Church), in reality it was a labour of liberating the Christian life from the narrow confines of a conventional religiosity and providing it with the motivation necessary for a genuine witness in collective and individual life.

It is highly significant that all these factors are a means of linking the Gospel, and the Church that preaches it, to the concrete realities of a particular time and place. The history of Brazilian Protestantism indicates that there was in this country a crucial moment of encounter between the Church and the world around, a true *kairos* for a vital thrust that was wisely (maybe spontaneously) used by an alert Church that had enough flexibility and freedom to mould its life and mission to the challenges of the hour.

But now in this new hour this 'adult Protestantism' is intensely involved in reflecting about its own structure and task. This has been determined by new circumstances and challenges that seem to demand new answers and new solutions if this Protestantism is to maintain its past level of relevancy and effectiveness. We would like to mention some of these new challenges.

The need is felt of developing new forms of communication and of community life that are more relevant to the 'ethos' and to the sociological conditions current in modern Brazil. This almost universal problem takes on special urgency in this country. Accustomed to being a Church that is growing and expects to grow, conditioned by its recent past to a sense of self-confidence, there is today a sense of frustration in many who are aware of the weakening aptitude of the Protestant Churches for adding new members. The reduction, and in some cases paralysis, of the rate of growth is a fact that we ought humbly to admit. The statistics of one of the Brazilian Protestant Churches of the 'adult' type (but a Church by no means the weakest in zeal for evangelism) reveals that its rate of growth in the last twenty years has only kept pace with the rate of national population increase, and that in recent years, in some regions, it has even fallen behind the national growth rate. We believe that the situation in some other historical Churches is not very different. Besides the increasing difficulty in the recruitment of new members, there is the problem of the exodus of some very significant groups from the Church. Some of the most alive and sensitive elements, particularly among the students and people of searching mind and heart, lose interest in the Church, some even in the name of loyalty to Jesus Christ, alleging that they have not found sufficient motivation in the witness in the forms of worship and in the style of life of the Church. More important even than seeing the weaknesses to which these facts and criticisms point is to hear the questions they are posing, even when we admit that numerical growth can no longer be the criterion for evaluating the vigour of Brazilian 'adult Protestantism': can this Church avoid the dangers of senility and nostalgia for its splendid past? Can it regain sufficient flexibility to develop, with all the risks that this undertaking implies and with all the confidence and faith that it confers, new patterns of life and mission, at the same time authentic and relevant?

The participation and involvement of the Church in the evolving Brazilian historical process is a second question that occupies an important position in the reflections of the vanguard of 'adult Protestantism'. These reflections do not deal only with the matter of being an 'indigenous' Church in the sense of concerning itself with specifically local problems or of being impregnated with a mentality and a theology that incorporates the perplexities and expectations of the Brazilian people, but also and mainly with being a Church that is capable of seeing and confessing the lordship and the action of the Sovereign God in the turbulent events of contemporary Brazilian history, and capable of responding in obedient commitment to this lordship. In a nation marked by ideological conflicts, the involvement of the Church in the march of events is a risky adventure which can bring into the Church itself tensions of all sorts in regard to basic doctrinal and ethical issues. But it is also the way to manifest the uncalculated loyalty of the Church to its Lord, and a truly mature disposition on the part of the Church to assume its own responsibility in the building up of the nation.

The question of the unity of the Church is being seen not so much in terms of the acceptance of the conventional principles represented by the ecumenical movement, and even less by means of formal affiliation to the World Council of Churches. Besides the remote influence of ecumenical thinking of our time, some quite independent and local factors are helping 'adult Protestantism' to discover the living fact of the whole ministry of the whole Church. Similar to other young nations in our modern world, Brazil is a nation in feverish search for nationhood, by means of an integrating power. This political concept of unity makes even more vital and urgent the witness of unity and reconciliation of the people of God, in spite of the inherited or native confessional or other diversities. The different branches of the Church begin to perceive more clearly that the consciousness of being branches from the same trunk and members of the same body is not only an interesting theological insight, but that it is an indispensable affirmation of faith that is essential to vitalize the message and the witness of the Church in the nation-making process of Brazilian history. On the one hand, new and promising possibilities are opening up for expressing this unity in the field of social service, evangelism and theological education. On the other, though, more progress is needed; for example, the integration of the laity in the mission of the Church ought to be expressed not only through the clericalization of the laity (which is common among us), but also in the recovery of the sacred meaning of the secular professions.

The future of 'adult Protestantism' resides to a great extent in the response it will give to these questions of structure, involvement and unity. For this purpose this Church will both have to reflect on the vital facts of its environment and meditate in a theological way over biblical events that are significant for its situation. The Brazilian Protestantism that has come to be known somewhat disdainfully as 'the religion of the book' is seeking today, at least in its thinking vanguard, to incorporate a more dynamic conception of the Gospel message of the living God in the Holy Scriptures that will move beyond the antiquated categories of either modernism or fundamentalism, categories that now and then still appear in some circles, in spite of their anachronism.

The two forms of Protestantism that we have been considering in the final portion of this paper have their own as well as reciprocal responsibilities. Their own responsibilities because, while 'young Protestantism' ought not to fail to recognize the precariousness and incompleteness of its work and witness, 'adult Protestantism' ought to liberate itself from the possible symptoms of sclerosis and avoid the absolutization of its hallowed traditions and forms. The diversity of gifts makes itself evident in this context and it is important to accept this fact seriously in a situation of cultural and sociological heterogeneity such as ours. Also, a common language of internal dialogue must be developed between these two types of Protestantism, a recognition of their reciprocal value and of the complementary character that they have in relation to each other. And this ought not to be done solely for pragmatic purposes, but in obedience to Jesus Christ and better to proclaim his lordship.

Great sectors of the Brazilian population show distinct signs of the so-called process of dechristianization. This results from the secularization of life under the impact of social change on the one side, and on the other from the tremendous growth of sub-Christian religiosity. Marxist philosophy and certain Afro-Brazilian religions seem to be offering more comprehensive and more immediate answers to the anxieties and problems of many than the Christian Church. In the city of São Paulo alone, for example, there are more centres of Umbanda, or primitive spirit worship, than there are Protestant churches of all denominations. Some of these facts should concern us deeply and honestly. But let it be said, to conclude, that these are signs of our time and place that may indicate a new *kairos*, a new unprecedented hour of mission and witness for the Church of Jesus Christ in Brazil. This new hour will demand, it is certain, a renewed Church, with a renewed understanding of the will and love of Jesus Christ for 'the sheep without a shepherd'.

b. Helping Churches Grow

THE MISSIONARY CHURCH

Jean Kotto

WE do not intend to give a definition of nor even a speech on the history of the mission of the Church in the world down the centuries. Our purpose is to witness quite simply to the work of our Church, 'the Evangelical Church of Cameroun', in its mission as a Church which gives concrete expression to its faith and radiates its message of salvation by means of evangelism among its members and outside.

The first missionaries to begin evangelical work in our country settled on the coast, the inland areas being still practially inaccessible through lack of communications. It was only in 1908 that the missionaries from the Basel Missionary Society penetrated Bamiléké, one of our regions on the inland plateau. This work had hardly begun when it was interrupted by the First World War, to be resumed much later by the missionaries of the Paris Missionary Society, together with the three Cameroun pastors in the locality.

Bamiléké numbers between 500,000 and 600,000 inhabitants, including, in 1959, 23,000 communicant Christians and 13,500 catechumens in our Church, and about the same figure in the Roman Catholic Church. Since 1959 our country has known one of the worst periods of its history. A reign of terror, slaughter and cruelty has swept the land, sparing none. Bamiléké particularly has been a prey to these regular outbreaks of murder and pillage, in which homes, hospitals, schools and churches have been set on fire and destroyed. More than two hundred of our churches and chapels have been destroyed. Pastors, evangelists and teachers have been killed. Our 1961 returns show 13,000 communicant members, and no catechumens to speak of, in the whole of Bamiléké.

The cause of these disasters can be found only in the sinfulness of those who do not know Jesus Christ. A population of more than 500,000 heathens in revolt! Convinced, therefore, that the cause of the rebellion lay first and foremost in the fact that these people have not heard the Gospel, our Church decided to launch, at the risk of our lives, a large scale evangelistic campaign. It was truly an act of faith, which surpassed human capacity and goodwill, a real mobilization of

a whole Church setting forth in the service of its Lord. The decision
was taken and preparations begun. An appeal was launched in Europe
for the help of missionaries specialized in evangelism. An evangelistic
commission was set up to organize the campaign. Cards, with subjects
for daily prayer and involving the holder in regular prayer, were
drawn up for wide distribution among church members and outside.
The general theme of the message was 'Jesus Christ, the Light of the
World', and was worked out as follows for use at public meetings:

a. Every man is a sinner; the wages of sin is death (as you can testify
yourselves!).

b. Jesus Christ accepted condemnation on the Cross in our stead
(with practical illustrations adapted to the situation, but which cannot
replace the ransom of redemption).

c. Jesus Christ by his Resurrection calls us to a new life (a happier life,
in this world, a life of peace in this land, of pardon and reconciliation).

d. The decision: 'Here I stand at the door and knock.' 'I present to
you life and death, choose!' 'Today, if you will hear my voice,
harden not your hearts.' Other messages suitable for youth and for
children were prepared.

The whole Church had become aware of its responsibility to
convert this tribe. In every parish, prayer meetings, special services,
devotional retreats were organized. The Church was already getting
impatient, finding these preparations too long. But this emotional
fervour had to be restrained to make way for the influence and wisdom
of the Holy Spirit. After all these preparations, the evangelistic campaign began in a certain area. The long-awaited moment had arrived
at last. All the presiding members of the Church were present, as well
as the Theology School with its students and the pastors and elders
who had come from other parts. And here was the campaign under
way after months of preparation. In teams it proceeded from village
to village, spending a week in each. The members of the teams had
no arms, nor military escort; but they went everywhere, into the
resettlement camps and into open country; no hut was overlooked,
no social class left out, even in the chieftain's quarters, the real village
strongholds. 'We were like hunting-dogs,' wrote one pastor, 'we
covered miles on foot, but we did not feel tired, we were not even
hungry; we forgot ourselves and pursued folk even into the fields!
Everywhere we were awaited and received with respect, as messengers
of the Lord. Everyone listened to us with joy, showing in this way

their acceptance of the Gospel of Jesus Christ, the Light of the World. What are we to do with all these pagans who are coming to us and putting their names down to be catechumens? We haven't any catechists!'

In the daily programme there was a brief time of meditation and recollection, early in the morning, and division of the groups. Then off they went, to reassemble, in theory, at noon for food and rest. But in fact this never happened. (You cannot make a time-table for people moved by the Holy Spirit nor for those who are touched by the Gospel and follow you!) They started again at the beginning of the afternoon and came together again at four o'clock on the public square of the suburb or village. Wonders! These public meetings were attended by thousands, tens of thousands of people; we had to resort to loud-speakers to make ourselves heard. Public testimonies were delivered, registrations were heavy. Bibles and Bible portions were sold to those who could read. There was singing and dancing in the joy of the sinner who has found peace once more: 'the people that walked in darkness have seen a great light'.

The teams were followed and upheld in prayer during the campaign by the parishes. The members were relieved every month. We received calls from every village, asking for the campaign to visit them, even those villages which were more or less out of reach because of terrorist hostilities. Not just a dozen villages, but hundreds of them; we shall need at least two years to get round them all at the present rate and with the density of population in each village. Here is an extract from a report written by a member of the evangelistic team in July 1962:

> How can words or figures express the extent and power of the Holy Spirit at work in the hearts of all who have heard the Gospel message? It must be told, however, that about 8,000 people have given in their names, wanting to follow the way of God.

Many areas have opened and admitted the Gospel where nothing like this ever happened before. What joy and consolation have been brought into the hearts of this people still subjected to atrocities and fear! Many administrative authorities have paid positive tribute to the influence of the evangelistic campaign in restoring peace in the area. If Bamiléké is now enjoying a time of peace, pardon, reconciliation and hope, it is largely due to the message of salvation carried there by this evangelistic campaign.

Difficulties: difficulties have not been lacking; one had to expect them. But they have been trivial ones. One chief refused us admission into his domain in spite of the wishes of his people. In certain parts, some Jehovah's Witnesses have spread counter-propaganda trying to oppose us—without success, however. The Roman Catholics distrusted us at first, fearing that we might draw away their followers, but finally came to understand our aim. And in certain places they have even joined in; one cannot really talk about difficulties. Pagan resistance to the message of salvation, however violent at the start of the discussion, would finally give way before our conviction in our message. These are not people who refuse the Gospel and cast it aside; rather it is the Church, with its obstinate fundamentalism and Pharisaic casuistry, which closes the door on them.

What are we to do with these thousands of pagans who have decided to follow Jesus? The existing and newly-built annexes are full of catechumens. Elderly people and the sick cannot get themselves to church three times a week for three years before baptism. The evangelists on the spot are overworked and others are necessary. And this three year catechumenate is obviously a long time for those of declining years and even for the young ones who run the risk of getting tired and giving up. Many other pagans in their thousands are wanting to join the Church, which does not admit this type of people. These questions of general order are those which we are facing now.

This evangelistic campaign has breathed a new spirit into the heart of our Church. In almost every synodal region revival movements are at the flood and are bringing many back to the fold, lapsed Christians, non-Christians (more than 600 new members in one parish alone). In addition, this campaign has forged the unity of the Church in a country where tribal entity makes for division. Lastly, pastors from other Churches have come to co-operate with us for the very first time in this evangelism and we have learned to know one another.

We should generalize a little too much if we were to speak of an overall enthusiasm. There have been faltering hearts, those who counted the enormous expenditure which this campaign would entail for the Church with its impoverished resources. Others were concerned about their safety and would not take any risks, excusing themselves with all they had to do in their own parishes and claiming that evangelism was the task of the Western missions who should be called in. There may well be among us here those who would make the same remarks; there are certainly those who are hesitant, calculating, fearful and troubled. What are you doing about evangelizing your country? What are you doing, each one of you, as a Christian, that is to say, as a bearer of the good news? Our thankful cry goes up to the Lord, and we beseech God to grant us his wisdom and the power of the Holy Spirit to nourish and establish the faith of these thousands of men and women who have responded to his call.

PROPHETIC VISION
IN THE EVANGELISTIC EXPRESSION
OF THE PROTESTANT CHURCH
IN LATIN AMERICA

Alfonso Lloreda

Translated from Spanish

IN contrast to a proselytizing attitude, there is in Latin American Protestantism a prophetic urge to witness to the different ethnic groupings.

Due to the fact that it is commonly believed that over ninety per cent of the Latin American Evangelicals have a Roman Catholic background, all Protestant evangelistic effort has been lumped together and maliciously accused of a petty proselytizing effort, which, hungry for numbers, has used all means including defamation in order to convert bitter and resentful Roman Catholics.

We accept the charge, for unfortunately many local and foreign evangelists, unable to express positively the grace and mercy of God in the Gospel, resort to destructive criticism of the Roman Catholic Church. Nevertheless it must be stated that the most successful expression of evangelistic effort has not been proselytism, but rather the indigenous motivation inspired by the Gospel of Jesus Christ to the end of eradicating some deep-rooted evil in the community. The ancient Hebrew prophet saw that, in spite of the existing prosperous and popular religious expressions, there were deep-rooted evils, about which the priest refused comment, perhaps because in its indifference such religion was impotent to solve them.

I

In 1934, an Otomi Indian of the Mezquital Valley, not far from Mexico City, bought a Bible from the mailman, having paid for it the high price of a sack of corn and ten golden pesos. Swiftly, and not yet knowing the meaning of salvation in Christ, he burned his books of magic, thinking that the Bible was superior. He heard the Gospel from a northern traveller who unfolded the message to him upon noticing the Bible.

'When I understood the Gospel,' says Don Venancio, 'I thought that the Otomis, who for a long time suffered humiliation at the hands of the whites, would be able to find their freedom.'

He began to proclaim that in Jesus Christ the time for their freedom had come. Being a farmer, he taught those of his own race how to make the land produce. Urging them to be baptized in the name of the Father, Son and Holy Spirit, he inspired them to pray for good harvests, teaching them responsibility for the tender care of their land in clearing it, planting and watering it, for it was a blessing from God.

'While God was redeeming souls,' continues Don Venancio, 'he was redeeming the dry land as well with the best harvest of wheat, tomatoes and corn ever seen in the Mezquital Valley. All for the welfare of my people.'

Concerned about the disastrous results of the great consumption of alcoholic beverages (made out of *lechuguilla*, 'little lettuce', a shrub of the maguey family), Don Venancio sought to find the method and equipment to change the negative industry of the *lechuguilla* into a prosperous cloth factory, using the same shrub.

'Now the brethren go out of the Mezquital Valley with truck loads of cloth, because the Lord has redeemed also the *lechuguilla* which was the cause of their degradation. It is an inspiring sight to see them weaving on home-made machines created with Don Venancio's help.'

It is astonishing to see that thirty years of Don Venancio's labour, under God's inspiration to free his people from the bondage of centuries, have resulted in an evangelical community where the ancient, miserable and dirty palm hut has been replaced by the house with large windows, bath-rooms, electric light and running water.

Four thousand converts, scattered through the valley and surrounding mountains, worship in twenty-four congregations, each one with its own pastor, and a beautiful church building which they have erected themselves. Upon seeing their vigorous effort the Government has decisively helped them by opening roads, building bridges to improve their commerce, reconstructing their town and bringing water and electricity.

Don Venancio established trade schools where bricklaying, mechanics, carpentry, knitting and dressmaking were taught. Above all, he taught his people to develop a deep faith in Jesus Christ and a great love for the land.

'To halt the young people's leaving for the city,' says Don Venancio, 'we must give them skills that will provide sufficient income to get married here and continue in their faith.'

This may be the reason why, when asked about the size of his congregations, he does not answer in terms of individuals but rather he will say forty, fifty or sixty families according to the case, identifying them by homes and by types of work.

On becoming aware that tuberculosis threatened the children, he taught the congregations their biblical responsibility of caring for and protecting them, promising to look for milk goats and chickens to enable the families to feed their young more adequately. He succeeded in doing so.

But the highest evidence of what his vision has done for his Otomi tribe is shown by the impressive reaction that his name and that of the evangelical community arouse among friends and foes alike.

Don Venancio, in need of land to divide among his people, knew of twenty-five hectares being sold for 305,000 pesos ($1.00=12.50 pesos). 'Don Venancio,' said the owner, 'if you vouch for it, I will give you the land and equipment, provided you pay for it within six years.' Having accepted the contract, he divided the land among twenty families, owing only 45,000 pesos at the end of the fifth year.

A man? No, an Indian, a humiliated and maltreated Otomi who, exalted by the Gospel before the powerful owner, was trusted with land valued at more than a quarter of a million pesos on his word of honour. When one is close to this man, there is a feeling of being close to a great prophet, whose soul has been invaded by concern for the destiny of his people and by the faith that Christ has as much power to redeem man as to redeem the land, the intoxicating shrub, the hut, and tuberculosis—thus creating a new environment for the new creature.

A study of this personality would give useful information to those who are trying to learn the best methods in evangelistic endeavour.[1]

II

Another example. Around 1920, a Colombian high school graduate from Cali became a Christian as he was preparing to go to college.

[1] C.A.V.E., the Audio-Visual Evangelical Centre, has filmed the work of the Mezquital Valley with realism and beauty in a twenty minute picture.

On receiving the Gospel he had the vision that his people, sunk in ignorance, superstition and fetishism, could, through the same process, come out of that depressed state in which they found themselves.

Giving up his studies he began to travel from town to town on foot, horseback or whatever means he found available, always carrying a load of Bibles.

'They live as they live and do what they do because they lack the light of the Gospel,' he said, 'but they will know the truth and the truth will lift them out of their darkness, . . . vision, action and words remind us of the great concern of the prophet Hosea: "My people err because they do not know God".' With the enthusiasm of the neophyte, this young man took the Bible from town to town, up to the villages on top of the Andean mountains, down to the valleys and the extensive hot, barren plains of the Colombian West, not counting the perils of hunger, illness or persecution. Indeed a sower of the message of light.

Everywhere he went from house to house, setting up Bible study meetings wherever possible, introducing the sacred book as the only source of the revelation of God's love and mercy and Jesus Christ as saviour. He stayed in each village the necessary time to fill it with Bibles and inspire the people to continue studying it. His passion for public discussions allowed him to show that the Bible had enough light to fight ignorance, superstition, idolatory and all the evils that harm the home and the community.

As we came to those regions twenty-five years later, there was no town big or small where 'Don Hernán', as he was called with affection, was not known and remembered.

We found fifty-three congregations comprising some 2,000 members, biblically trained to support themselves through tithes and gifts and to help in the construction of their church buildings. Everywhere Don Hernán taught new methods of fighting insects, achieving better harvests and above all, achieving a strict puritan and disciplined Christian character.

More than thirty years of prophetic vision allowed Don Hernán to prepare the fields where many Protestant denominations found ready ground for the establishment of their work, witnessing to the solid foundation prepared by this servant of God.

Unfortunately later missionaries, in order to give ecclesiastical form to their work, dispensed with Don Hernán's methods, destroying thereby something that had grown naturally out of the perseverance of a man consecrated to Christ.

III

A living legendary figure of the plains of Apure in Central Venezuela received the Gospel through a colporteur in 1924. Because the Gospel had taken away his prison-like vices and sins, he thought the same liberation was possible among other similar lives. With a puritan and demanding John the Baptist type of message, Don Arístides, Bible in hand, went with enthusiasm throughout the Venezuelan valley to end sin and vice.

'During my brief stay in Venezuela,' writes the Rev. Henry Strachan in 1939:

> I had the privilege of helping, although insignificantly, in the work of the different Evangelical groups in Central and Western Venezuela. Although I was highly impressed by the advancement of the Gospel brought about by the zeal of the workers, the thing that impressed me most was the results of the zeal and consecration of brother Arístides Díaz, whose daring work produced some 2,000 converts and sympathizers.[1]

'It was on August 8, 1927,' reads Don Arístides' testimony of 1939:

> that the Lord told me to 'go and preach the Gospel'. My wife, Felipa de Díaz, and I, defying winter's cruelty on oxen carts or on a boat, sought souls. The first tabernacle that the Lord used in these valleys was a place under the tree 'merecure', this being my first meeting on September 8, with an attendance of eighty-five persons who are now members of an Apure Church.

He sums up his effort, writing in 1939:

> The work increases day by day with nine chapels finished and others on their way. Apure has forty congregations. How has this happened? The Lord has used the Apurean Indians, who, notwithstanding danger and privation, have been moved by one desire: the salvation of souls.

Much is being said pro and con about his work. Evidence shows that after thirty years of labour there is a prosperous Evangelical

[1] Translated from *El Mensajero Biblico*, 1939, p. 3.

Church with eighty-five organized churches and as many congregations; eighty church buildings erected by the Indians, comprising some 6,000 members ministered to by some sixty pastors trained by Don Arístides. 'Indigenous Apurean Evangelical Church' is the name of the work, the result of a profound Evangelical faith. Bethel, where Don Arístides lives, is an entirely Evangelical community with a school and hospital attended by Evangelical teachers and doctors, free of vices and managed according to the Bible. 'Calvin in Geneva and Don Arístides in Bethel' is the humorous saying of the locality. His loud voice and strong character embody his unchanged message serving the vision of Isaiah that we all from the top of the head down to the feet are but a single and rotten sore; and that the Gospel has power to take away sin and the vices that enslave us.

To men like these, super-individualists if you like, with the patience and perseverance of deep convictions tested under all conditions, with a prophetic vision of their mission, we owe, more than to the apologists and proselytizers, the great increase of Protestantism on our continent.

HELPING CHURCHES GROW

John V. Taylor

'GO,' said Jesus, 'and make disciples of all nations.' To whom were the words spoken? To the first Apostles, yes. But we believe they are a charge laid once and for all upon every humblest member of the Apostolic Church. These words are our credentials and our authorization for world mission and evangelism.

Yet we cannot pretend that we stand today where those first disciples stood. From that upper room they looked out upon a total world-ignorance of Christ. If they did not carry the Gospel to the nations there was no one else to do so. They alone were the Church. But today, as this Assembly in Mexico City testifies, there is a Church in most parts of the world. What then? Does this exempt our generation from that world-wide responsibility which once rested on every Christian? Is the task of evangelism today a matter of 'You in your small corner and I in mine'? Or are we bound, one and all, by that original mandate and still committed to the ends of the earth?

There are several ways of answering these questions. Certain missionaries and their supporters still manage to think and talk and act as though Christ's mission rests in their hands alone. I have seen an article, for example, in which the writer said: 'Here we have ninety communicant members. My nearest partner in the Gospel is two hundred miles away.'

At the other extreme is the school of thought which would restrict the foreign worker to technical and specialist tasks on the grounds that evangelism and pastoral care can be effectively carried on only by the indigenous Christians. Someone in Rhodesia once said to me, 'Mission work, as distinct from Church work, means schools and hospitals.'

Each of these attitudes falls far short of that fellowship in the Gospel which alone is adequate to meet the opportunities and challenges of this moment. The true pattern, surely, is that of the fishermen who, under the blessing and guidance of Jesus, found it was too much for them to haul in so great a catch of fish. Nets were tearing, the edge of the boat was borne down almost below the waves. So, we read, 'they beckoned to their partners in the other boat to come and help them.' (Lk. 5:7, R.S.V.)

The reason why we have failed to realize how much we need each other is that we have forgotten what the Church's real work is. Simon Peter and Andrew did not call their partners for a pleasant sail round the lake, nor even to help them paint their boat or patch their nets. They needed them for one reason only—to help them haul in the fish. They did not call them over as experts or specialists but simply as partners, because the job was too big for them to cope with on their own. I have not a shadow of doubt that when any Church anywhere in the world begins to tackle seriously the main job for which it exists, to bring its own neighbourhood, its own nation, its own society to the saving grace and lordship of Christ, it will immediately and without question come to know its need of partners from elsewhere.

I could point to one situation after another in my own country where it is becoming patently clear that British Christians on their own can never meet the need. However faithful and enthusiastic our mission to our own people may be, we are too stale, too much taken for granted, too burdened with our own history, to be able to break through with newness and surprise. And the very essence of the Gospel is surprise. We must call in the partners the Lord has given us.

Not many weeks ago I called on the minister of a London church in a depressed area. I knew that in his parish there were about equal numbers of British, Arab, Pakistani and Caribbean residents. He and his two assistants were making very little headway. We walked round the dingy streets and I talked about the possibilities of a team ministry. I suggested we might appeal to the Churches in Pakistan and the West Indies each to contribute a missionary. I said I felt pretty certain that before long, when neighbouring churches saw his mixed team of workers in action, they would want to share in it and he might have to be ready to break down the parish boundaries, and the confessional boundaries, and release the vitality of this new joint witness into a wider sphere. A week later he wrote me a short letter saying—and I quote:

I have had great searchings of heart since your visit and feel that God has done much to increase my vision and my faith as to what he will do through us as we fully obey his word. Indeed, this experience has been something very much akin to a second conversion.

That is what can happen to an almost defeated man when he catches not more than a glimpse of what the Church's mission might be in this age of interdependence.

I was able to talk to that man with some conviction because I had seen that kind of partnership working in quite a different context.

In Northern Nigeria, for example, there is a mixed team centred on the city of Bida and working among the Nupe people in a multitude of little walled villages all round. The team leader is the senior pastor of the district, himself a Nupe. Under his discipline the team prepares itself, with a daily morning worship in his little chapel. It is he who takes in hand the language study of the foreign members and, whenever he is at home from his pastoral visitations in the district, calls them together for discussions of the work. His regular team includes a younger Nupe clergyman, two evangelists and several leaders of women's groups, two English women trained in adult education and a married agricultural extension worker. In the first three months of every year they go out to a chosen area for a dry season campaign taking with them as many others of the regular church leaders as can leave their homes. From their headquarters in one of the larger centres they cycle out each morning to some tiny village where they begin to drum and dance. Dancing, by the way, is something the four missionaries have had to learn with their language study. In a short time almost all the villagers have crowded round to watch and to join in. Then they begin to sing—Christian songs adapted from traditional Nupe lyrics, interspersed with little bouts of preaching. After an hour of this the group breaks up and chatters with the by-standers, answering questions, joining in the laughter, showing concern for local news, sympathy with any in sickness or misfortune. Then they move on to repeat the whole performance in a second village before the midday meal. After a rest they go to a third place, returning in the evening to their headquarters to discuss the day's work over supper and show a filmstrip, perhaps, or a little play after dark. When the three months are over it is time for sowing and everyone wants to get back to his farm. But before they leave the district there is always a deputation of village headmen, most of them Muslims of a simple kind, sent in from all around, 'You cannot leave us now. You have brought us good words, everyone is talking about it. We want to hear more.' That is the chance for the permanent members of the mixed team, especially the foreigners who have no other responsibility to tie them down. So through the next months there is a steady follow-up, with Bible teaching and literacy classes, supplemented with the practical compassion of informal rural development—some help with sick children, advice on simple hygiene and farm improvement. Year by year new congregations are coming into being and a request has been made for another foreigner, an ordained man to help to train those who are chosen as ministers of these congregations, a man who will also become a good linguist with skill to operate a small printing press so as to produce immediately whatever reading cards, Scripture portions or other literature this rapidly growing Church may need.

There are many similar areas in Africa and elsewhere where primary evangelism is still being carried on in such simple terms as those. But it is not always simple and direct. The crowded cities of the world, especially the centres of new urbanization, call for the proclamation of Christ in highly skilled and tough-minded ways. The people of the city who have been bewildered and broken by it are for the most part bitterly unattractive; those who are not broken, and there are many more of them, have a hard and happy self-sufficiency. They are Christ's lost sheep, but a sentimental shepherd will not last long in this concrete wilderness.

One such place is Port Harcourt in Eastern Nigeria. Its dynamic energy and its frightening problems are a symbol of a hundred other new cities. In five years its population has swollen from 40,000 to well over a quarter of a million. Like a magnet it draws tens of thousands of village boys in search of the jobs which will never exist. One typical factory this year had 150 jobs to offer and the management received 30,000 written applications.

In the old town there is a close cluster of different churches but they are symbols of the past and their hard-pressed staffs cannot cope with the human tides that have engulfed them and are tempted to clamber up on to their own little rock of safety. But they have not done that. Three years ago the Anglicans and Methodists called to their aid two women from Britain to start a social welfare service, and offered them a Nigerian girl as colleague. One of these soon entered the Government social service locally, where she has remained a staunch ally, and was replaced on the church team by another missionary. Clubs were opened for girl delinquents, a marriage guidance council was established, a beginning was made with prison visiting and a remand home and a small social centre were built. One multiracial, interdenominational congregation restored and reopened a derelict seamen's club in the port area. But this was only scratching the surface. Then last year, under the leadership of the Nigerian bishop in Port Harcourt, a local Planning Committee of the Churches was formed and a great comprehensive scheme of new centres and new initiatives was worked out. Again they beckoned to their partners and at their invitation an expert in industrial evangelism went out from Britain to help them with the detailed plans. Today there is an entirely new courage abroad among the committed Christians of Port Harcourt. They are preparing to locate more of their own best men in new posts in the city and they are looking beyond Nigeria for a port chaplain, an industrial chaplain, a trades-union worker, two health visitors, a probation officer, a psychiatric social worker and an adult education officer, every one of them not just a skilled professional but in the deepest sense a committed evangelist. These folk and their Nigerian colleagues will need housing and some community centre or clinic to work from. It is a vast programme, a massive appeal. But that is only one city of many, strung out along the coast-lands of West Africa. And there are many, many more 'Port Harcourts' in every other continent.

Do we shrink from the task because it is so great, because it is no longer simple, because it demands a skilful, protracted effort at understanding and identification far beyond our strength and our ability to love? It is a good thing to be frightened by the things Jesus asks us to do, if only that it drives us back to our need of him and our need of one another. For the miracle of the great catch of fish is still there for us. If we really have him, and if we really have one another, we have everything—everything the world needs.

c. *Meeting with Men in the Cities*

MEETING WITH MEN IN THE CITIES (i)

Harry Daniel

I WISH in many ways I had to give this talk a few years hence—for to me, 'meeting men in the cities' is the challenge and not yet an accomplished fact. That is not to say that this meeting will ever be accomplished in the final sense—for it is a continuing process of meeting and rejection, of meeting and reconciliation, of meeting and shying away, of meeting and encounter.

What I have to say will bear the marks of one who has recently moved from student work to parish work, of one who worked as National Student Secretary in the Student Christian Movement and then as a parish minister at the Cathedral Church of St Mark's. What follows will therefore be limited to Bangalore, to St Mark's and our own feeble efforts at mission.

The City

Many towns and cities in India have grown up in a more or less unplanned way. There are many backgrounds for the origin of our cities: ports where people gather for trade and commerce; forts or military headquarters with the army and its attendant retinue; temples of fame and importance and the community that grows around them; Government seats with the attendant offices and staff; industrial growth and the establishment of new factories and estates.

The decade 1941–51 recorded the most spectacular growth in towns and cities due, of course, partly to the impact of war, partition and independence. But the decade 1951–61 recorded the lowest rate of urbanization during the last five decades, in spite of rapid industrialization. This may be due to a number of reasons such as decrease in refugee migration, reaching of saturation point in the cities, progress in rural areas, development of the region around cities and surplus labour in urban areas, etc.

It is too early to predict the trend in the present decade. The only factors that should be mentioned are the large number of young men who are joining the armed forces since the emergency, and the expansion and establishment of factories related to defence, which is absorbing more workers.

Towns have grown up through the amalgamation of villages or the spreading of towns absorbing neighbouring villages, and most of these are therefore unplanned. There are also other cities better planned, like Bhilai which has grown due to new industry, or Chandigarh due to the establishment of a new administrative state capital.

Bangalore bears the marks of a number of these factors. It was and is a military centre, the seat of the state government and is now the centre of growth of a number of industries due to the availability of hydro-electric power, a good climate and the encouragement given by the Mysore State. Prior to 1940 Bangalore could not be called an industrial town though there were a few textile mills and a few State Government industries. Growth has been recent. At one time Bangalore was the pensioners' paradise with a good climate and cheap food. Industries have now started—four central government industries— aircraft, telephone, machine tool and electronics alone employing about 40,000 people. The City Improvement Trust, co-operative housing and industrial estates cannot cope with the housing demands of the population which has doubled in the last ten years to about two million. The cost of living is increasing each day. Migrants are moving in from neighbouring villages and neighbouring states in search of employment. Bangalore today is a city of extremes—parks and open drains, mansions and slums, employed and unemployed, the rich and the poor.

People with different cultural and caste backgrounds and habits find themselves living in the same neighbourhood. The city is increasing in size day by day and life is rushed and conditioned by time. There is overcrowding with acute problems of shortage of water, housing, transport and other civic amenities.

Changing Patterns in the City

What held Hindu society together was the caste system, the joint family and a system of law. All these characteristics are undergoing rapid changes largely due to industrialization and urbanization, as well as to the influence of leaders like Mahātma Gandhi and the new legislation of independent India, for example the abolition of untouchability, the new marriage laws, control of Hindu religious endowments, the place of women and community development. But Hindu society has the amazing capacity of resilience under pressure. Over a hundred years ago it was thought that Western higher scientific education would destroy Hindu society. But this has not happened. Some people feel that industrialization and urbanization will destroy the institutions that hold Hindu society together. It is an amazing fact that Hindu society finds it possible to adapt itself to social changes and the Hindu religion is reinterpreted to meet the demands of a new scientific industrial era. However much this may be true, technological changes are producing social changes. Let us note some of these changes which are characteristic of the city.

a. Diversification. One no longer finds one caste in one locality. This voluntary isolation in housing was noticed in villages and in older towns. But it is breaking down in the new industrial areas. In one locality many caste groups are found and, especially in the factories, a man may find himself working under and with men of a lower caste —a vegetarian working with a non-vegetarian, a Hindu working with a Muslim. There is therefore in the city a real meeting of different cultures, religions and habits. However superficial this meeting may be, it does broaden the outlook of the people.

b. Family. A man moves away from the close joint family and caste system when he moves to the city. In times of crisis like death the whole village or at least the joint family and caste would rally round him. In the city he finds himself alone. Joint families were a great cushion against the ravages of domestic crisis and an orientation for the new wife beginning her married life. Though money wages are higher, at times of financial crisis a man has to write home to his village, for it is a rare city neighbour who will share his earnings.

The place of women is undergoing a radical change. This is due partly to higher education among women and partly because women find it necessary to supplement the family income by working, owing to the higher demands in standards of city living. When the woman is also a wage-earner her attitude to the man changes. There is a greater degree of equality of status than the man has been accustomed to. This is also true in the field of parent-children relationship. At school children meet and go to the homes of other children who are wealthier and therefore have more amenities of life, such as the radio. The children tend to say to their parents if they cannot afford a radio they should not put restrictions on their spending greater time in the homes of their friends who have radios. The source of authority which was understood and respected in the past is now undergoing change in the direction of joint consultation and decision. In the midst of these tensions everything returns to a joint family bliss during the occasional visits of the old folks from the village. These are some of the tensions of a city nuclear family.

Rash statements that a man in a village sees his bride for the first time on the day of his marriage are not always correct. In the joint family-caste system the bride in all probability was the neighbour, a girl with whom he played and quarrelled in childhood. The families were known to each other and in the joint family there were always the older folk who helped the young couple in the period of earlier adjustment. In the city even a married man has to come alone to the town to seek work and to find accommodation. It is sometimes many years before he can bring his wife and children to the city. This lone existence creates many emotional problems. If he is a single man he may strike up friendship with his women colleagues and fall in love and get married. Many of these marriages are inter-caste and inter-religious marriages, which sometimes lack the undergirding factors necessary for a happy marriage.

In the city, owing to electricity shortages, there is a staggering of weekly holidays. This is particularly true of Bangalore. Many find themselves in homes where father has a Monday holiday, Mother if she is working in another factory a Thursday holiday, and the children in school Saturday and Sunday holiday. Apart from the difficulties of Sunday worship for Christians this poses to many families of all faiths a real problem of the family never really being able to be together.

c. *Conditioned by Time.* Seasons and the weather of the village now give place to the clock with the hours and the minutes. Factory work is to a strict time schedule. The town man is time-conscious and also overtime-conscious. Life is busy and there is the rush and scramble of city life. Some of the smaller factories complain of absenteeism which is due to the village way of life still finding its place in the cities. This time-consciousness produces nervous tensions and heart diseases. Relationships between people have also become formal and time-conscious.

d. *Fragmentation of work.* The unity of the village disappears in the city. There was an integration between a man's faith and his work, his pleasure and his life. Today in the factory he performs partial repetitive tasks, due to the higher degree of specialization within industries. He does not see the entire process or the final product. He has little or no contact with the consumer. This often does not give meaning and satisfaction to the work he is engaged in.

e. Basis of Choice. A man in the city is selected for a piece of work on the basis of skills and aptitudes which he shows according to the requirements of industry rather than because of his caste and traditional ties. A supervisor in a factory is tempted to bring others from his caste or village to the same industry. If today there is nepotism in the cities it again goes to show that village patterns of life die hard.

f. Means of Production. The man engaged in industry has to work with complicated machines and intricate tools which he did not conceive and make and for which he is responsible without owning them. He often thinks of them in the same terms as the village plough, especially at the time of the Ayudah puja. Even this does not give him any sense of mastery over the tools of production. The gigantic machines which are important in industry have a new sense of awe for him. But he also sees that machines depreciate and get redundant and so are replaced by more modern and up to date machinery. A time comes in his own life when he sees himself as another tool in the industrial process to be replaced by others.

New Emerging Values

In the light of what has been said one can see new social patterns emerging as a result of city and industrial life. It would be facile to assume that these patterns are leading to a new crystallization in attitudes and values. Indian culture seems to have the unique quality of allowing the coexistence of differing patterns without finding the need to do away with any one of them.

Having said this, let us look at some of the positive values which emerge in relation to man in the new cities of India.

a. Secularism. Man has become conscious of the immense power put at his command by the conquest of nature. The domination of man over nature which has been rising imperceptibly for thousands of years, all of a sudden has taken a vertical curve upwards. Each new discovery leads up to more gigantic unsuspected possibilities. He sees that this conquest of nature can be made to serve and bring prosperity to all men. This faith has quite subtly led him to a secularism which sees value and meaning within the structures of everyday life with no reference to a supra-natural faith. Many of the city dwellers observe a lot of old religious ceremonials but this observance has less meaning than it had before. These ceremonials have more social significance than faith significance. There is a new affirmation of the material.

b. Solidarity. Man sees the creation of the new world as the collective task of the workers all over the world. Modern work, understood in this wide sense, implicates man in an increasing network of human relationships of co-operation and communication. These have reached world-wide dimension and given birth to a new concept of solidarity. The consciousness of participating in a great common enterprise for building a more human and just society has great attraction for men. There is also a sense of sectional solidarity because of conflicting interests. Workers see their solidarity with fellow workers in a trade union. But this is not confined to workers alone. There are groupings of managers, teachers, doctors and traders, etc. The success of collective bargaining gives man a sense of greater confidence in this new solidarity. The presence of power structures gives man a further justification for solidarity and collective bargaining. Rights are no more the gift of overlords, but rights have to be struggled for and won by the underdogs or maintained by those who at present are in possession of power.

c. Selfhood. Man in a new way is realizing his selfhood. He is slowly freeing himself from subservience to nature. In science and technology, as seen in the industries and the life around him, the man in the city is coming to feel the power of man over nature. With less dependence on nature and the natural forces and with a greater dependence on the machines and tools that he makes he is coming to a greater respect for himself and his powers.

As the joint family gives place to the nuclear family he is also thrown on to himself, since he has to take responsibility for his family's sustenance, education and protection, and make important decisions in its life, for example, in marriage. Similarly with the decreasing help he gets from his caste in matters of jobs, status or influence, he finds it necessary to develop his own skills and powers. Also in the midst of the solidarity of unions and associations he is seeing a new potential for finding justification and power for his rights as a human being.

The Church

There are churches in Bangalore over a hundred years old. A number of these churches were established by the then British Government to meet the needs of the British army and personnel and were supported by the state till Independence. Missionary societies also established churches. But the growth in churches continues. Every Church is engaged in putting up new church buildings in the new suburbs of the city.

There are some negative characteristics of the Church which should be noted.

a. Conservative. The Church continues its same pattern of worship and work. One sometimes feels that if the Church of England ever lost all copies of its 1662 Prayer Book it could come to some of the ex-Anglican churches in the Church of South India and find its service preserved entire and celebrated the same way as in 1663! What I am trying to say is the Church seems to have changed so little in spite of all the changes around.

b. Sheltered. Though the priest and lay members of the Church are very much in contact with the life of the world, yet their faith and the life of the gathered community bear no relationship to the meeting with the world. It seems so easy in the life of the Church for lay men and women to forget the world from which they come with all its joys and hopes, its pressures and frustrations and to fit into a religious ethos unrelated to the life of the world.

c. Dependent. Though the churches that once received Government grants are now independent of that source of income, it is surprising to see how dependent we are for our ministry, institutions, etc., upon money from foreign missionary societies. In spite of all talk of partnership, there is a great deal of colonialism. One sometimes feels that we are ruined not by the maliciousness of foreign mission boards but by their good ideas which the Church in this land has not learnt to appraise and agree or disagree with. Much of the fault for this is due to the Church in this land not trying to discern its own calling and mission, and seeing what things need to be done and how they should be done in a joint venture with resources from India and abroad. The pattern of secular and inter-governmental collaboration has much to teach us here. Maybe Joint Action for Mission is one attempt to correct this. Dependence of a certain nature is deadening, as there is in this dependence a desire to please someone or to conform to some pattern, rather than to obey the living God and to accept the structures that he suggests.

d. Institutions. Many of our institutions were started and initiated largely by foreign missions and still continue to receive support from outside. Our schools, colleges and hospitals cater for a large percentage of those who profess other faiths and these institutions provide a sense of power and prestige to Christians far out of proportion to the numerical strength of the Christian community in India. What their future is in a developing welfare state is a big question. There is little thinking about new patterns of service that the Church should render to the life of the world.

e. Clergy-Centred. Apart from church committees the congregations tend to look to the clergy not only for the running of the Church but also to initiate new work, keep contact with the life of the world, undertake evangelistic activity. The clergy also tend to look upon the laymen as raw material to help him in his clerical function, and for the running of institutions in the life of the Church. The sad fact is that the laity accepts this and any anti-clerical quarrels are usually for the wrong reasons.

f. Divided. We are divided denominationally. Churches are tempted to rush into new industrial areas for the sake of denominational dividends. In city churches one still notices caste patterns and power struggles between old and new migrants, often based on caste and denominational difference, especially in a united church where there is a great mixing of such people.

The Christian

One notices three types of Christians:

a. Those who have been born in a Christian home to whom faith has no living reality. What they do on Sundays is conventional and this has no bearing on the workaday world and they have a completely different set of values for this world.

b. Those who have a deep personal Christian experience. They are concerned about converting their neighbours. If the neighbours are not willing to listen to them, they distribute tracts hoping that these will be read. Their neighbours think of them as fanatics and kill-joys. They have a strong personal morality but do not see their rôle and place in trade unions or the way a group works in social and power structures. They will not collaborate with others who do not think like them even for the limited goals for which one has to strive in industry.

c. Those who are churchmen who are beginning to think out the implications of their faith in relation to their work and life, and these get very little help from the present life of the Church.

However much the Church seems to fail in the present missionary task to which it is called, there is a great allegiance to the life of the Church as it is, and with very little demand from the laity for any basic changes. This is because:

1. The lack of change in the life of the Church makes the Christian who comes to the city accept the Church as the one institution he knew back home in the village. In the midst of all the change this is the one institution that seems changeless. He is accepted here as a person. The Church is concerned about him, with his family and also in his new potential as a church member and a church giver. The priest visits him in his home and he knows he can call on the priest at times of crisis. This gives him a certain new strength and status in the midst of impersonal town life.

2. There is value in the fellowship of the Church. This he experiences not only in the worshipping congregation but also in the many smaller fellowship groups organized under the auspices of the Church.

3. The Church, partly because of its institutions and partly through its lay members in positions of management and responsibility, has some influence in the securing of jobs, etc. Therefore as an insignificant individual a man finds it worth keeping on the good side of the Church, at least for his own ends.

4. The Church is one place where a laymen who may not be too significant in the industrial hierarchy can seek power in church committees, and exercise some authority over the priestly manager!

5. In choosing a particular church the language in that church and the cultural background of the worshippers plays a large part.

The Task

The real task is the task of meeting—of meeting the living Lord and recognizing him actual and alive in every sphere of life, of meeting him and hearing his word of judgment and mercy, of meeting him in one's neighbour and recognizing that all which is good in him is because of him.

Meeting involves a twofold task:

a. Collaboration with God in his creative purposes. This involves helping to give direction to men in their mastery over nature. It is no use pointing out the dangers of industry and technology in developing countries. We should share with men the enthusiasm of the administrator, planner, engineer, scientist and the worker. All this is of God— the Creator God. God created all things and is continually present in all the creative activities of the modern city. The Christian, therefore, should individually and corporately involve himself in the life of the world.

b. Collaboration with God in his redemptive purposes. This involves the Christian in helping the world to use its mastery over nature to the true benefit of mankind. It involves helping men to be reconciled with one another both as individuals and as groups. He is a God who loves the whole world and died for it. In the life of the Church there is the new community, in spite of man's sin. In the Sacraments we have a foretaste of the Kingdom of God. Our laymen must be helped to be true ambassadors of Christ in individual relations and social actions.

In this the Church requires a specialized ministry and it is in this context that we have just recently begun the Industrial Team Service as part of the ministry of St Mark's Cathedral. We have been in existence as a team for about three months now. It is too early to say anything definite; that is not to say that anything definite will emerge even after five years. But there are pointers in the work:

1. As a beginning, the usual Harvest Thanksgiving service was changed to portray also some of the industries and five-year plan publicities in Mysore State. In the chancel and sanctuary were cycles, telephones and component parts, sandalwood and silk manufacture, oxygen and small scale manufacture. It made people think. Many of our worshippers have promised to bring more industrial produce next year. Of course these had to be returned to the industries after the service and could not be used in the church auction after the service, nor could we give them away to the poor as we normally do, but it did help us to bring to God in thanksgiving and intercession the industries of Bangalore.

2. A group of managers and workers have met regularly once a month for about three years trying to understand what it means to be 'salty

Christians' in the life of the world. Even if we have not achieved much they have enjoyed Christian fellowship. Our Christian workers have just begun to collaborate with Roman Catholic workers in a possible programme of co-operative housing and co-operative credit.

3. An East-West dialogue has begun with Indians and foreign technicians who have come to Bangalore, helping each group to understand the other and we hope that what the Church was not able to do in their homeland we may be able to do in Bangalore.

In the light of this experience we have at present a threefold aim: to care pastorally for the needs of the new growing industrial townships around Bangalore in providing them with worship and Christian nurture; to help laymen and equip them for their apostolate in the life of the world; to study, to understand and to engage as Christians in the power structures of modern industrial life.

In our meeting with men in industry here are some typical reactions:

1. A group of managers wanted to know why the Church was interested in the industrial sphere and what it hopes to achieve as a result of this. They are willing to hear us further if we can show results in terms of industrial efficiency and growth.

2. A person connected with left-wing trade unions wanted to know why we are concerned and whether we ought not to continue with more prayer meetings, distribution of tracts, etc. He even said that those of them who had no religion would value our prayers.

3. One trade union president would like the Church to continue its services with hospitals and schools in the new industrial township.

The average manager or worker is concerned about himself earning and living and wanting to make more money. What the Industrial Team Service is striving for does not appear to the man in the city as being of immediate relevance, but we must continue the meeting of men in the city, for it is only through this that Christ and his purposes can be openly confessed, so that man may worship not the Ba'al of yesterday but the living God.

MEETING WITH MEN IN THE CITIES (ii)

George E. Todd

I COME to our topic from three kinds of city experiences: a New York City inner-city slum, a rapidly industrializing and urbanizing Asian situation, and now a United States national mission office with responsibility for developing urban church strategy.

In East Harlem I worked in the middle of one of the United States' decayed inner-city areas. Here have been caught men and women who have never gotten their feet on the escalator of North American affluence. Decayed housing, disease, inadequate schools, crime, family disorganization, juvenile delinquency, narcotics addiction, all combine to trap thousands whose children and grandchildren have little prospect of moving up or out. (They represent the two fifths of U.S. population which live in poverty, deprivation and need.)

From there I went to work with the Church in Taiwan. Taiwan's story at most points parallels the story Harry Daniel has told us about the social revolution transforming a traditional rural, agricultural society into a continually changing urban, industrial society. The ten largest cities in Taiwan have doubled during the past twenty years. One has trebled and one has quadrupled in population. In 1951 there were 5,000 factories in Taiwan. Today there are 29,000. During the past four years, at the invitation of the Presbyterian Church of Taiwan, I have had an opportunity to participate with that Church in seeking and shaping structures for a continuing study and understanding of social change in Taiwan, and in a search for forms of church life obedient to what God is demanding of the Church there for ministry and witness to men within an urbanized society.

Recently I have returned to the United States to the staff of a national missions board. From this standpoint one sees the United States as an urban nation. Men do not live simply in cities. They live in metropolitan regions, entirely urbanized and thoroughly inter-dependent. America's eastern coast from Boston to New York to Philadelphia to Baltimore to Washington is one great urban region. Seventy-five per cent of the United States' population lives in these

75

metropolitan regions. The Presbyterian National Missions Board, with other similar departments through the National Council of Churches' Division of Home Missions, addresses itself to how the Church performs its missionary responsibility in an urban nation. Beyond this national missions question, our department, in a home missions board, works closely with the Commission on Ecumenical Mission and Relations of our Church as it responds to urbanization all around the world. Forty per cent of the world's population will live in Asian cities by 1975, a United Nations report tells us. Mexico City has increased in population from one and a half million to five million since 1940. Fifteen fraternal workers, trained at the Institute of Industrial Relations of the National Missions Board, and with work experience in home missions in American cities, are now at work in ten nations. Harry Daniel and other foreign visitors are bringing their experience, evaluation and criticism to bear on our work in North American cities.

Our topic tonight, *Meeting with Men in the Cities*, has for me an active meaning. It suggests that the Church is to go out from its own ground into the city, to where men are living and working, to meet them. A passive meaning pictures a church building, bearing a sign saying 'Everyone welcome'. The church members wait inside, prepared to offer a bow or a handshake, if any stranger should venture inside.

We have great hesitation to meet men in the city on other than our own ground. Even when we make more active efforts to meet them, we call conferences of laymen at our own retreat and conference centres. We make institutes and study centres, to which we bring men from their life in the city for meetings on our own ground, about economics, politics, science, in places where we can set our own terms for meeting.

I want to offer three ways, or modes, in which the Church should be meeting men in the city, on the city's ground.

1. We should meet men in the cities in their strength at the places where the city is being built, where decisions are made, where men do their work. The Church must be a discerner, affirmer and celebrator of God's sovereign and redemptive activity in the structures and institutions of urbanizing society where men live and work.

2. We meet men in the city with a vision of what God wills for the city in his continuing creation. We meet men with a vision of God's New Creation which we are told is a New City. The Church with

such a vision must be a source of articulation of norms and values, aims and goals, for men in the city.

3. We meet men in the city where they are flagrantly sinning and flagrantly suffering. The Church must be a cross-bearer in the midst of the city.

Some urban churches in the United States are engaged in testing their own faithfulness in the city by asking: (1) Are we meeting men where they are at work shaping the life of the city? (2) Are we meeting men with a vision of what a city might become? (3) Are we meeting men where they sin and where they suffer?

I

The Church knows, as the world outside the Church does not, that Christ is Lord of the city. He holds the city in his hands. He is actively at work there, governing, creating, redeeming. The Bible passages we have been studying illumine directly our view of the city, its life, its institutions. Colossians' word: '. . . in him all things were created, . . . whether thrones or dominions or principalities or authorities— all things were created through and for him . . . and in him all things hold together.' (Col. 1:16–17, R.S.V.) Or Ephesians: '. . . far above all rule and authority and power and dominion, . . . he has put all things under his feet . . .' (Eph. 1:21–2, R.S.V.) These are affirmations that Christ is Lord over the city government, the police force, the public school system, the state university, the factory, the bank and the labour union. They all have their being in him. Romans 13 tells us the governing authorities that exist have been instituted by God and have no authority except from him; that the tax collector is a minister of God, ordained for this very ministry. This chapter is talking about the mayors, city councilmen, policemen, superintendents of schools, labour union officers, factory managers, bank presidents and newspaper editors in our cities. The Church knows, as these men may not, that they are vested with authority for ministry in the city.

The Church approaches the power structures of a city and meets men within it as an affirmation of its faith in the active lordship of Christ presently at work within these structures and through these men. We approach them, not to take God to them. Knowing God is at work within these structures and has a will for them, we go expecting to discover there what shape our own obedience to God in the city should take. Rather than deciding first on our own ground what God's will for us and for the city is, we are called to look for and listen to what our faith tells us that he is already at work doing in the city.

In Formosa, during the past several years, groups of Christians have taken initiative to go in quite simple ways to meet men in their cities, in the places where they exercise their power. A series of conferences have been held, with programmes designed to bring about this kind of meeting.

After a brief introductory lecture, members of the conference divide into groups for going out into the city. Small teams go to the city government buildings, the police station, the public school, the government health station, the labour union office, a large factory.

In the city offices Christians discover God is at work through a non-Christian mayor who is seeking ways that the city can minister to aged, children, and handicapped, who are left without care as the larger family system disintegrates. From the chairman of the council of trade unions and from the chairman of the city economic development committee they have glimpsed God at work in their city, providing jobs for men, making possible the production of goods for a fuller life, creating new possibilities for greater justice in wages and working conditions for labourers. They ask how citizens might serve in helping meet these needs. In these encounters they discover a shape of Christian obedience being written for them by what God is already actively doing in the structures of that city's life outside the Church.

A Christian women's group was worried when they approached the city government building in one city to find the traditional Chinese red greeting banner over the door, bearing the words, 'Welcome Christian Women. Please come in and advise us.' One woman said, 'If we ask officials the questions on this list, they might expect us to do something to help them solve problems and meet needs.' The leader indicated that this was the very point!

As these groups come back to the conference at the end of the day to report their experiences, they come with quite concrete ideas for action, for Christian obedience in the city, opened up to them in the midst of an encounter with men at work shaping the life of the city.

At Tainan Theological College this affirmation of faith that Christ is Lord of the city, that Christians can expect to meet him at work there and to discover patterns of obedience for themselves there, has brought some new dimensions to training for the ministry. Orientation of new students now includes an introduction to the city where they will be spending six years. The field work programme of the school includes one year of what is being called 'world-directed' field work. Each student must spend one supervised year in a part-time practical work assignment which takes him into an entirely secular setting to work among non-Christians, or with Christians in their lives outside the congregations.

Some 'world-directed' students were assigned to become acquainted with labour leaders in their city. Through this kind of contact students learned about the contribution of the labour union to the development of the economy and to the welfare of workers in an under-developed nation. After a year of such contact, the union officials approached the students, asking help in developing a labour education programme. They said, 'According to state laws we should be carrying on a programme of labour education. We don't know what this means, and we don't know how to do it. We can get state funds to assist with this programme. We have people and we have space, but we have no programme. Can you help us?' One of the students was sent to attend an International Labour Organization training school for labour educators. He learned techniques for helping workers understand how to use their labour unions as instruments to improve their working conditions and to improve labour legislation. Although he is still a theological student he is actively at work helping unions in that city develop labour education programmes there. This pattern of Christian service and obedience was opened up in the midst of meeting men in the cities where they live and work.

Some Formosan churches have been understanding that vocationally self-conscious Christian laymen represent a major dimension of the shape of the Church meeting men in the city. If you should inquire about the work of the Presbyterian Church in Chaiyi City, you will be told, as you would in most cities of the world, how many churches, how many members, and how many children in their Sunday Schools there are. But you will also be told, there are so many doctors, so many public school teachers, so many industrial workers, so many students.

Several presbyteries have made a vocational census of their members. One presbytery discovered that although only two per cent of the people in that area were Christians, thirteen per cent of the public school teachers, and forty per cent of the doctors, were Presbyterians. Over two hundred barbers were Presbyterians. In these areas Christians have begun to meet regularly in vocational groups. They meet, not so much to stimulate more participation in 'church activities', but rather to seek better understanding of God's will for them in their daily work. Barbers, asking what God's will was for the barber, to what ministry in the city he is ordained, answered, 'God has called us to the ministry of making men clean and beautiful.' Barbers, traditionally having a very low status in Chinese society, decided that Christian barbers had a particular responsibility to conduct their business in ways that would upgrade the low status of the barber in Chinese society. They recognized the rôle of the barber's shop in urban society as one of the places where men meet. They talked about the way their shops were decorated, about the language and conversation of the barber's shop, and about the ethics of the use of women barbers as an important aspect of competition between barber's shops.

Christian government employees expressed a great sense of relief to be able to air for the first time, within the context of the Church, with honesty, the anxiety and tension they feel from their involvement in a system in which bribery plays an important rôle.

One 'world-directed' theological student does his field work as a part-time employee of the daily newspaper in a large city. He has tried to discover what journalism as Christian vocation means, and how the newspaper might more adequately perform the task of acting as a conscience in the urban community. By self-conscious application to this task during one year, he was able to more than double the space which that newspaper gave to social issues in the city. Through the columns of the daily press, he was instrumental in bringing to the attention of the whole community places in the city where people were suffering physical deprivation or injustice.

The first mode of meeting men is to seek encounter and involvement in the midst of daily work where we may meet God, where we respect and uphold those who are God's instruments, and where we discover what our own obedience is to be as citizens and as workers.

II

A second rôle the Church should fill as it meets men in cities is to go to men of the city with a picture of what God wants of a city. What does God mean a city to be? What is his will for a city? The Church has a rôle in articulating within the city ideals and norms which picture what a city might become, and aims and goals towards which a city might be moving. In most cities this kind of vision, of what a city might be, is offered only by writers of tourist literature, chambers of commerce and city government public relations officers.

In our first morning's Bible study Philip Potter spoke of exertion of physical and intellectual energy apart from any act of the will. Tremendous physical and intellectual energy has been invested in the building of our cities, yet it is not inaccurate to say that most of our cities have not been shaped and developed according to deliberate choices made in favour of some idea of what a city should be. Physical and intellectual energy to build cities is not exerted by acts of will. Our cities have just grown up. Forces not comprehended by any deciders and actors have shaped our modern cities. The development of industry required concentrations of labourers. This stimulated the building of urban housing, not with a view to making the city a place of gracious habitation for men, but to shelter at the lowest possible investment and with the highest possible hope of profit the new factory workers who were compelled to come to the city to find jobs. Technological development of transportation, blessing us first with the railroad train, then with the automobile, has determined basic features of every large modern city. Decisions about efficient moving of men and goods from place to place have been made without consideration for the effects the placement of roads, highways, railroad tracks, bus and streetcar and elevated lines have on the possibilities for a fully human life in the city.

The result has often been that we have abandoned as impossible any hope for a full and human life—a life in which the intentions for man, made in the image of God and put in command over nature, might hope to fulfil—in the city. We have been hypnotized by the dehumanizing qualities of a city as it continues to grow according to apparently autonomous forces.

Many a Christian in the United States has rejected the city for a suburban home, carrying in him an ancient peasant longing for a piece of land of his own, where in his own yard he can live an abundant life with his own family, unbothered after a hard day's work in the city by the city's crowds and traffic or by the sight of, or responsibility for, those whose poverty or colour will not let them leave. He takes no personal joy in common ownership of public parks and gardens and fountains, museums and libraries which he must share with other men. We have had a Christian bias against cities, viewing them in the biblical images of Babel and Babylon and the prophetic denunciations of Jerusalem. But Lewis Mumford, a secular humanist, in his book, *The City in History*, gives us a different picture of the city. He says that cities are meant for meeting:

. . . the city should be an organ of love; and the best economy of cities should be the care and culture of men.[1]

John Oman, a Christian sociologist and historian, describes world history as an urbanizing process. He sees urbanization of society and the urbanizing of men as the desirable end towards which history has been moving, as the hunter and the nomad and the farmer have founded villages and towns and cities. He speaks of the civilizing and humanizing vocation of the city and calls for an 'urban teleology' that might set forth and hold up before us a vision of the desirable city (and city man) which is to be.

Is it too far-fetched to see in biblical history a story of a divine urbanization process? The Bible does tell us that here we have no lasting city. But what we are to seek is not a rural refuge, according to the passage in Hebrews. It is the *city* which is to come. We have a Book which begins with one man and one woman dwelling in a garden. The Book ends with a city in which all men and nations are reconciled. Is the building of cities a working out and fulfilment of God's first command to Adam, 'Take dominion over all the earth, fill it and subdue it'? The biblical vision of man's future is not restoration to a garden but fulfilment in a city. Man's destiny is seen to be the abundant life, fulfilled in the meeting of men of all nations in a city. The kings of the earth do bring the glory and honour of the nations into it. The Revelation to John describes the skyline in detail. Not rough stones and ore of primeval nature, but cut and polished jewels and refined gold are the building materials. The details may sound rather gaudy for modern tastes, but the picture is of an architecture raised to glorify God and to provide spacious mansions for the inhabitants. In this vision we learn that the saints are destined to become urban men.

[1] Secker and Warburg (1961), p. 575 (U.S. edition, Harcourt, Brace and World, Inc.).

Mumford writes:

> The city first took form as the home of a god: a place where
> eternal values were represented and divine possibilities revealed.[1]

Jerusalem was such a city.

The Church has a mission to help men see what cities are for and
what they are meant to be. David Barry, Director of New York City
Mission Society, in a lecture at a Board of National Missions meeting
of Presbyterian urban church workers, said:

> It is possible that the best contribution the urban churches could
> make right now is to try to state as precisely as possible what
> they understand God's purposes to be for the urban centres in
> which they minister.

Then he tries to state it for New York City:

> God is trying to show us that people of all nations can live to-
> gether, not only in mutual respect, but in mutual enrichment.
> He wants us to discover that by appropriate division of labour,
> training and specialization, the individual's talents and powers
> can be released for undreamed-of accomplishments; that this
> metropolitan structure can produce a wonderful variety and
> diversity. He is helping men in cities learn that the imaginative
> use of finance can be a tremendous boon to humanity. He is
> telling us things about the flowering of the human spirit in art
> and literature and culture. He is providing a theatre for all the
> governments of the planet to work together for mankind's
> release from all kinds of bondage. He is providing a gateway to
> new dignity for minority groups. All these, and much more, are
> part of God's plan for this city.

In every large metropolitan centre in the United States today, the
Church is pursuing active dialogue with the men who are making
decisions about the shaping of our cities. The Church is pointing out
that, in making a city, enriching the possibilities of human meeting and
loving and living must take priority over concerns for moving cars
in and out of cities rapidly, or for increased technical proficiency in
production of goods, or the commercial profit possibilities of land use.
Under the leadership of the Division of Home Missions of the

---

[1] Op. cit., p. 575.

National Council of Churches in the U.S.A., working with denominational home mission agencies, a new kind of ministry has been rapidly
developing. A growing number of clergymen, with training in
economics, sociology, urban planning, social research, as well as with
pastoral experience in urban (usually inner-city) churches, are now at
work in positions with titles such as Director of Urban Church Mission,
or Director of Strategy for Urban Missions. These specialists are
engaging persons in the power structure of a city—political leaders,
technical experts who design urban renewal projects, superintendents
of schools—with questions about the norms and values according to
which they make their decisions, the ends and goals towards which
they are striving, in their shaping of the city. The Church does not
have the competence to tell city planners just what shape the city
should take, but it does have some competence to call them to freedom
from a technological and economic determinism which commits
them to exert physical and intellectual energy apart from exercise of
will in choice of alternative ways to fulfil values to which they are
consciously committed.

   The Church Federation of Chicago is engaged in carrying out a
proposal developed by Stanley Hallett, Director of Planning for the
Church Federation. The project proposal says:

> The religious institutions have a central focus on the basic values
> and norms which undergird, not only the whole society, but each
> of the dimensions of society. The religious institutions ought to
> be geared to generating thought and discussion and debate about
> the future development of metropolitan Chicago.

A panel of specialists and generalists is exploring alternative possibilities for the future of the Chicago area. He says:

> This would include an examination of decision-making structures,
> and basic questions about goals, norms, probable developments
> and feasible alternatives.

Such a panel might include persons from the fields of theology,
ethics, sociology, law, economics, anthropology, political science,
education, science and technology, labour, history, communications,
management, finance, housing and urban renewal, social welfare,
land-use planning and philosophy. The effort is being made to develop
a picture of alternatives for the basic institutional structures of the

metropolitan area, and images of what the society will look like assuming different sets of basic norms. Through the Division of Home Missions of the National Council of Churches, this proposal is currently being shaped into a nationwide proposal for action by major mission boards in the United States.

(As a citizen of a nation sending many technicians to other parts of the world for work which will accelerate urbanization in formerly rural countries, I must ask what rôle the Church in the United States has in stimulating responsible articulation of norms and goals in the world urbanization process.)

III

I have spoken about Christ, present active Lord of the city, calling the Church to meet men fulfilling their ministries in the structures of the city. I have spoken about the vision we have—the Christian hope of a city where men of every nation dwell together in harmony and righteousness, a city in which there is nothing unclean, nor any abomination or falsehood.

But we live now in this moment, in the cities, between the times—between the time of God's decisive redeeming action for his creation in Christ and the time of God's gift of the New City we long for. We cry out with the saints, 'Come, Lord Jesus', as we wait with longing, seeing all too plainly that sin and death and Satan are still manifest in the city and in us. The demonic use of technical knowledge, possibilities for manipulation and exploitation of men by men, the claims to autonomy by institutions and by some professions, the fear and the suffering and the hatred, and the separations between men, all lead contemporary Christians to join the cry and the affirmation of Hebrews 2:8-9 (R.S.V.), '. . . we do not yet see everything in subjection to him. But we see Jesus . . .'

The Church is called to a third mode of meeting men in the city. The Church must meet men in the city where men sin and where men suffer. The Church must meet men in the city as a cross-bearing Church. The Church, as the body of Christ in the city, is called to take upon itself the sin and the suffering of the city. The Church is called to the imitation of Christ, who did not count equality with God a thing to be grasped but emptied himself, taking the form of a servant. For our sake he became sin. He became obedient unto death.

The Church in the city is called to imitate Christ in its exposure to the city at the points where men are most flagrantly disobedient and where men are most acutely suffering. In the United States today any church stands condemned (and the pastor is a false shepherd) if that church is not actively taking upon itself the pain of the nation's sinful racial discrimination, and is not pouring out its life, offering up its body, to fight for elimination of discrimination in housing and employment and education, and to struggle for a city in which all men may live side by side in equity and brotherhood.

The city church, called to imitate Christ in the city, is often a middle-class church, with an educated ministry and a respectable membership, comfortably clothed, housed and fed. The Jesus we can see in the New Testament picture, this Jesus we are called to follow, is the man who made an active practice of entering into relationship with the physically unattractive, the blind and lepers. He met the prostitute and the dishonest politician. In every picture, and there is one after another, Christ meets these men and women with acceptance and forgiveness, offering new life. When we see Jesus meet the socially, financially, religiously secure, his words are always harsh: 'It will be very hard for you ever to get into heaven. Sell all you have and give it to the poor. Woe. Woe. Clean on the outside, filthy inside. White-washed tombstones.'

Cross-bearing is not a major shape in which the Church can be discerned in our cities. But here and there are individual Christians or congregations standing beside the unemployed, the aged poor, narcotics addicts, juvenile delinquents, taking up crosses where they are raised in the midst of the city. Here and there churches are risking their lives in challenging the structures of organized corruption, crime, and injustice which cause suffering, and in attacking the structures which preserve indifference to suffering. The Church cries out, 'Thus saith the Lord! My will is violated in the city!'

In a number of urban communities in the United States today, where men without adequate shelter, employment and education have been powerless to let their needs be known and powerless to act to improve the condition of their families and their communities, the Church has quietly taken the lead in bringing people together to help them to articulate their just demands and to help them make their voices heard where decision-making power in the city lies. Enforcement of housing laws, improved and desegregated schools, clearance of old slum housing and provision of new houses for low-income families, improved sanitation and rat control, enforcement of fair practice from money-lenders, are part of a long list of signs of renewal brought about because the Church recognized, identified with and took on itself the sufferings of men in the city. In this form of service, ordinarily called community organization, Protestants and Catholics have worked together alongside non-churchmen, meeting men in the city as the Church engaged in a common effort to realize the will of God for human life in the city.

Christ tells us plainly enough in Matthew 25 that he is waiting to meet us in our cities. He calls the Church, absorbed in maintenance, upbuilding, nurture and extension of its life, to go out into the city, exposed to the worst that is there, offering its body and substance on behalf of sinners and sufferers. He stands in the city where the cross is raised, waiting to offer the resurrection life to the cross-bearing Church, waiting to welcome us all into his New City.

d. *Meeting with Men of Other Faiths*

WITNESSING TO MEN OF OTHER FAITHS

Sabapathy Kulandran

THERE are three questions round which a discussion of the subject of this conference will have to converge: the Why, the What, and the How of it. The first arises from a doubt; the answer to the second will decide whether that doubt is legitimate or not; and it is only if it is not that we can go on to the third.

The Why

A doubt as to whether we have a right to preach our Gospel to people of other faiths is a late-comer into the Church. There was of course some doubt in the matter at the start among the Palestinian Jews who were Christian (the Hellenistic Jews had none); but that doubt was not merely confined to a certain group or a certain area, it was technical and temporary. It was technical because, though the Palestinian Jews had come across many nations in their history and were even then living under the Romans, they had looked upon them almost as a part of nature, and had never allowed them to enter into their religious thinking. It did not strike them that these nations needed to be saved. The Palestinian Jews were living in a narrow intellectual world. It was temporary, because once Paul widened their outlook, that doubt was lifted from their minds.

In the long centuries that followed, doubt on the subject hardly reappeared in the Church; and neither in the Dark Ages, nor the Middle Ages, nor through the greater part of modern times did the matter become a live issue. The behaviour of the Portuguese, who came east in the wake of Vasco da Gama's discovery of the Cape route, might have laid itself open to question from many points of view; but nobody could have questioned their evangelistic zeal. And after the Reformation, as soon as Protestantism realized it was still alive after its life and death struggle, it began to send out missions in successive waves.

There have, of course, always been many individuals who for reasons of their own have disapproved of efforts to convert people of other faiths; but in each of these cases the reason has been particular and not general. For instance, Sydney Smith, the English clergyman and humorist, was always making fun of William Carey's efforts in Bengal; but he was also making fun of the Methodists and the Evangelical clergy in his Church. He was not grieved at Brahmins being asked to give up their faith; he was against enthusiasm in any form.

A general doubt in the matter may be said to have crept into the Church only in the twentieth century; and the explanation commonly given is that only now have Christians begun to realize that there are other great and enlightened faiths in the world besides their own; until now they have believed that all other religions were masses of debased superstition. Throughout the nineteenth century the great systems of Eastern religions were being opened up; and in this present century Christians have begun to feel the full impact of that new knowledge. The doubt of the Palestinian Jew was caused by living in a narrow intellectual world; the doubt of the modern Christian is caused by his living in a wide intellectual world.

The doubt that had crept into the Church became embodied a little more than thirty years ago in a movement of considerable momentum and expressed itself in such books as *Re-thinking Missions*, issued by a band of American thinkers headed by Dr W. E. Hocking of Harvard.[1] That movement was handled rather roughly by Hendrik Kraemer in his famous book, *The Christian Message in a Non-Christian World*,[2] and since then the doubt has expressed itself more mildly and with far greater hesitation. But however it might express itself, it is reasonable to believe that it will continue to exist in the Church as long as it has to face numerous closely reasoned and highly coherent intellectual and religious systems.

Does it mean then that ignorance can be the only sure basis for evangelism? Ignorance has been considered a basis for many things, including the universe itself. Writers from such widely divergent backgrounds as the great ninth century teacher of Hinduism, Śankara, and Bertrand Russell give no other reason for the existence of the universe. '. . . there is little but prejudice and habit to be said for the view that there is a world at all', says Russell.[3] Whether the universe likes to owe its existence to ignorance or not, ignorance as a basis for

[1] Harper Bros. (1932).
[2] Edinburgh House Press (1938).
[3] Bertrand Russell, *The Scientific Outlook*, Allen & Unwin (1954), p. 98 f.

Christian evangelism is quite unsafe. Ignorance is temporary; and is always meant to be displaced by knowledge. 'When the perfect comes, the imperfect will pass away.' The security of a narrow, intellectual world is illusive, because that world is now large and will become larger.

But those who think that an urge for Christian evangelism can exist only when there is ignorance about other religions must reckon, in the first place, with the fact that for long the Church's evangelistic efforts were directed to people whose faiths it knew, and not to people whose faiths it did not know. If there were many faiths it did not know, neither did it make any evangelistic efforts among those who professed them. The Hellenistic Christians who took the Gospel into the Graeco-Roman world knew that it was a world where Plato and Aristotle had taught; and they knew the various religions that had come into Rome from the various parts of the Empire. Origen, Justin Martyr and Clement of Alexandria knew all the systems that prevailed in their time. Yet they preached the Gospel. In the Middle Ages, when these religions had faded and Islam had swept into dominance, it became well known in the Christian world. The great Islamic universities in Spain catered for most European scholars of the time. The Islamic philosophers, Avicenna and Averrhoes, were held in high respect in Christian circles. If the Crusades did not express evangelistic zeal, they certainly enlarged Christian knowledge of Islam. The interest in that religion was sufficiently deep to produce a translation of the Qur'an into Latin as early as 1143 (though the book itself was published much later); and Martin Luther himself issued a German translation in the sixteenth century. All this knowledge did not create the slightest doubt in the mind of the Church as to whether the Gospel should be preached to Muslims. It may be seen, therefore, that ignorance did not in practice provide the basis for evangelism.

In the second place, if Christian evangelists in later times went out to preach the Gospel among those whose faiths the Church did not know, the fact must be reckoned with that these men played a major part in opening up these faiths to the world at large. B. Ziegenbalg, Joseph-Constant Beschi and Philip Fabricius opened up the Tamil language in the eighteenth century; and a host of American and British missionaries did so in the nineteenth. William Carey put out one of earliest Sanskrit dictionaries and translated the Ramayana in three volumes; H. R. Hoisington, G. U. Pope and Schomerus opened up Śaiva Siddhānta; Bishop R. S. Copleston was one of the pioneers in presenting Theravāda Buddhism to the West; and Nicol Macnicol in throwing light on the Hindu poets of Western India; more German names could be added to this list. It may be seen, therefore, that neither was ignorance regarded in principle as a basis for evangelism.

Again, whilst it has to be admitted that evangelism has often been carried on when there was ignorance of other religions, it has also to be admitted that more often it has been carried on when there was knowledge. Obviously then, though ignorance might coexist with evangelism, it could not be its basis. Therefore we must conclude that a knowledge of other religions may be an occasion for doubt about the legitimacy of evangelism, but cannot be its cause. Schopenhauer, the German philosopher, professed a sublime admiration for the Upanishads and for Buddhism, and affected a supreme contempt for Christian missions (refusing even to believe that they could have succeeded). But his attitude to the Upanishads and to Buddhism was not the cause of his attitude to missions. Doubt or certainty about the legitimacy of evangelism arises not from one's attitude to anything outside Christianity, but from one's attitude to something within it. Both arise from one's attitude to 'the What' of the Christian faith.

The What

All religions have certain common features: places of worship, rituals, priests, laws that favour order rather than disorder, customs and ceremonies bearing on social and domestic life, differing no doubt from country to country but suited in their diversity to the various places where they prevail. The tendency at the first sight of this fact is, therefore, to equate them all, and to account for their differences by the variety of their origin. This is what the Roman magistrates did: they found all of them equally useful. Peace-making on the basis of these common features is quite easy.

These features, however, in each religion cluster around certain affirmations about what is considered ultimate reality. The Graeco-Roman philosophers regarded all these affirmations as equally false; but they were asserted, and are asserted now, because they are considered true; and religions exist because they want to assert them. As against the Graeco-Roman philosophers, it is declared by the author of *Upon the Earth*[1] that no religious system is of purely human origin. Religious systems are vast and complex things and may contain great and noble ideas; but we are concerned with their basic affirmations.

The obvious difficulty about attributing all affirmations to divine inspiration is that often the basic affirmations of one religion contradict those of another: and God is a God of order and not confusion. Islam insists on the wide gulf between God and man. Hinduism identifies both as in the phrase, '*Aham Brahma asmi*' ('I am Brahman or God'). Buddhism denies the existence of both. To push the doctrine of the sovereignty of God to such lengths as to attribute divine inspiration to all affirmations is to push monism beyond itself, because monists are always arguing with non-monists, trying to convince them that they are wrong. When we want to fix responsibility outside the realm of human agencies, it is also scripturally unwarranted to fix it solely on God; St Peter makes it clear that outside that realm there are other agencies also at work.

Religions often coexist because of political necessity; but a concordat based on a mutual recognition of equality can be possible only on two grounds: either that of regarding their affirmations, though different, as not very important, or on the ground that opposites may still be equally true and be two sides of the same reality, meaning by this that as long as they are opposites they do not have real validity and do not amount to much. It is on the basis of the first that a recent Christian scholar of Buddhism takes up the well known Christian hymn, 'Immortal, invisible, God only wise' and sweetly suggests that if only we could leave out the word 'God' from the entire hymn, the Buddhists could fill it with such words as '*dharma*', '*karma*', 'Buddha' and 'Nirvana' (and we can all live happily ever afterwards). It is on the basis of the second that Hinduism is willing to accept every viewpoint, affirmation and religion, holding that at the level of reality differences do not exist. Therefore, the Bhagavadgītā makes Krishna say, 'Even those who worship other gods come to me', and Vivekānanda goes to the extent of saying that all religions are forms of the Vedānta.

It will, however, be apparent that neither of these grounds is a sound basis for a concordat. It might perhaps be asked how it is that the basic affirmations of a religion ever come to be regarded as

[1] D. T. Niles, Lutterworth (1962).

unimportant. The answer is that because of their importance they are put at the centre; and because they are at the centre, they are taken so much for granted that they often come to be overlooked, their very importance being the reason why they are sometimes allowed to sink into unimportance. But a concordat based on an oversight can be of little use. As for the other basis, if people would not like to build on an oversight of the importance of the central affirmations of all religions, they would like still less to build on the deliberate repudiation of the importance or validity of any affirmation. Hinduism, which invites us to do so, itself drove out Buddhism when it refused to accept its viewpoint. In practice Hinduism absorbs rather than tolerates. To ask religions for an enduring concordat between themselves that would ignore the importance of their respective affirmations is to ask too much of them.

From the time of Kraemer's second big book it has become customary to speak of the task of evangelism as basically that of producing an encounter between God and man. But God is always meeting with man in many different ways and in many different places. What is the task of the Christian evangelist? It is to make man meet with God in the life, death and resurrection of Jesus Christ. When the evangelist brings about this encounter, then indeed he is presenting the Gospel; that is, he is presenting the good news that God was in Christ reconciling the world unto himself: he is preaching the word. That word is a proclamation and is at the heart of the Christian faith. It constitutes 'the What' of the Christian faith.

A proclamation is also an affirmation; but is more than an affirmation. An affirmation may be general; an affirmation about ultimate reality may be to the effect that it is personal, and an affirmation about God may be about his being and nature. A proclamation is definite and pointed. An affirmation need not bear upon the immediate situation and therefore need not have any urgency; whereas urgency is of the essence of a proclamation. The Christian proclamation is that God has come in Christ and has saved man; it is news of an event, an event of cosmic significance, but with a bearing upon the immediate human situation. It declares how the Almighty, King, Creator of the ends of the earth has come down in a human being; how that human being has died for us and risen in glory; and how by saying 'Yes' to this event man is saved. From many angles it is quite incredible, but if it is true, all general affirmations about the ultimate reality dwindle into insignificance, if not irrelevance. It will mean that upon mankind's 'questions, its dreams and hopes and intimations, its discussions, its pitiful and fruitless efforts to win peace and purity and home', there now shines 'a light that never was on land or sea'. If such an event has taken place, mankind's age-long quest has ceased to be a quest, and the 'low, sad music of humanity' may well turn into a paean of triumph.

The event which the Church proclaims is not the fact that there was a human being at a certain place and time, that he did certain things and that certain things happened to him; but the fact that God was in that human being, and through the things he did and which happened to him, God was saving man.

It is the divine, cosmic significance of these that constitute the event which the Church proclaims. It is this significance which constitutes 'the What' of the Christian faith. If that significance is denied, the Church has nothing to proclaim. If we accept that significance, we accept that the event has taken place; and if it has, then we accept that the Christian Gospel must be proclaimed, no matter how many great religions there are in the world. A realization of the presence of other great religions actually does a service to the Church, in that it makes her examine what it is she wants to preach. It draws attention to 'the What' of the Christian faith.

That the existence of other religions does not bear fundamentally on the legitimacy of Christian evangelism may also be seen from another angle. If those who discover the fact of other religions claim that it unsettles their previous thinking, what about those whose thinking has always had to assume that fact? Neither my own father, nor my mother's father discovered non-Christian faiths. They were born in them. These faiths do not come upon our horizon as a sudden and unexpected phenomenon; they are the environment into which we are born. A professor from a Western country once told me that while he could intellectually defend the divinity of our Lord, he found it difficult to believe it in his heart. 'On the other hand,' I said, 'even if we cannot find intellectual arguments for it, we find it easy to believe this in our hearts, because without believing it we cannot be Christians at all.' The presence of non-Christian faiths serves only to sharpen the focus of 'the What' of the Christian faith in places where men live all their lives in the midst of them.

If there is no doubt about 'the What' of the Christian faith, there is not merely a legitimacy about Christian evangelism but an urgency. The daughter of Karl Marx once confessed to a friend that she had never been brought up in any religion and had never been religious. 'But,' said she, 'the other day I came across a beautiful little prayer which I very much wish could be true.' 'And what is that prayer?' she was asked. Slowly the daughter of Karl Marx began repeating in German: 'Our Father which art in heaven . . .' That God whose conceivability itself raises questions about his very existence should not merely exist, but could be called 'Our Father' is a profoundly consoling thought; but that that God should have come down in a human being, who 'has borne all our griefs and carried our iniquities' and has saved man for ever, transcends all human aspirations and all human imagination and endows all life with a new aspect. 'If I believe that Jesus Christ really died for me, I would not write or speak about anything else,' said Lord Morley, the atheist.

The commission to evangelize was given not in a world without any religion, but where there were many, where the Buddha had taught 550 years previously and where Plato had taught 400 years previously; where the major Upanishads had all been long written and where the Bhagavadgītā had been written well over a hundred years earlier. It must be preached not in spite of the fact that the Ālvārs, the Ācharyas and the Marāthā saints have sung movingly, but because of the fact that they have. Such a world is worth saving.

The How

The task of the evangelist is to proclaim the Christian message to men of other faiths. In view of the task given, it is therefore curious that the suggestion should be made that we should ignore these faiths to which these men belong. Those who make this suggestion usually take their stand on the saying of the late C. F. Andrews, who spent most of his life in India, to the effect that he did not preach to Hindus but to men. How many Hindus know their Hinduism, it is asked; so why not forget the fact that they are heirs to 3,000 years of Hinduism and just treat them as men, apart from all religious and philosophical predispositions and presuppositions?

With deference to the memory of a great and good man, it may be said that he was not coining a *bon mot* but committing a *faux pas*,

and a wide one at that. People do not have to read systematic treatises
to imbibe their ideas. John Whale quotes a very appropriate parody:

> Jesus loves me, this I know;
> For my mother told me so.

Men get their beliefs in a thousand different ways. Besides, while
many Hindus may not read Śankara and Rāmānuja, many read the
Bhagavadgītā and know the Purānic stories. Many Buddhists may
not read the Pitakas, but they know the Jataka stories and often listen
to the chanting of the Pirith at various ceremonies. These people,
therefore, have lived in the midst of Hindu or Buddhist beliefs and
worship and in the general environment created by these religions.
To think that all this has not influenced their beliefs and presuppositions
is scarcely realistic. They mould their will and shape their personality.
To think that we can detach a man from his beliefs and presuppositions
is to think that we can detach him from his own personality.

Neither is it realistic to minimize the part played by classical
writers and systems on people's beliefs. No doubt in every context
every man fashions his own brand of religion. Classical writings are
always studied only by a few; and perhaps were meant only for a
few. But their main teachings seep down into the religious and
intellectual heritage of races and communities. They may get modified
and adapted in many different ways, but they have a habit of persistence
and a gift of essential endurance. Classical systems in practice manage
to live on not in the books which are not read, but in the people who
usually do not read them.

It may of course happen that persons living in a Hindu context
may be persons of no-faith. But a no-faith is usually the reverse of a
faith and is influenced by that faith. Non-faith in the Hindu context
is usually Hindu non-faith. A Hindu gives up his faith and falls back
on astrology (which is the epistemology of *karma*) to guide his life.
When Gautama Buddha rejected the faith of Hinduism, it was its
reverse, its non-faith, that he adopted. Buddhism (Primitive Buddhism)
is unintelligible without Hinduism.

An eminent writer has recently told us that God is 'previous' to
us in the person to whom we preach. We cannot by any means
imagine that God's care for people is less than ours; but we have seen
that it is impossible to detach a man from his ideas and beliefs and treat
him as altogether separate. If the 'previousness of God' means that in

spite of all a man's preconceptions and imaginations, God still wants to save him, it is true beyond a shadow of doubt. But if the 'previous-ness of God' means that these preconceptions and imaginations are the 'clouds of glory' that God has trailed in his wake, it is scarcely acceptable.

The task of the Christian evangelist is referred to in the New Testa-ment by the word *kerussein*, which means 'to proclaim' or announce. But a proclamation on certain subjects and in certain contexts cannot be an instantaneous act; it has to involve a process. We see that the proclamation of the New Testament evangelists themselves did involve this process. They had to do what is meant by the word used, I believe, in most languages to translate *kerussein*: they had to preach; and preaching involves convincing.

Nowadays we are asked to enter into a dialogue. Perhaps preaching sounds too dogmatic, self-confident and intolerant. But the aim and method of dialogue are the same as those of preaching. Preaching may look like a monologue, but is essentially a dialogue. The listeners may not answer back, but if they are to be convinced, their unspoken objections must be inferred and answered.

A dialogue is very different from a conversation. The classical examples of dialogues are to be found in the writings of Plato; those of conversation in Boswell's *Life of Samuel Johnson*. There is no set purpose in conversation, and there are no set subjects. Johnson may hold the centre of the stage, may hold strong opinions on particular subjects and may want to put them across. But the conversation does not take place so that Johnson may put his opinions across. It starts incidentally from one subject and flits unpredictably to quite a variety of subjects, on which nobody may have definite opinions. In fact, we are told that Johnson often uttered various introductory phrases so that he might in the meanwhile decide which side of the question he should take. But in Plato, through page after page, by means of ques-tions and answers, Socrates is building up his argument.

Dialogues even on the same subject vary according to persons and according to the times. Those living in a later age can make use of a greater knowledge than those of an earlier age. Therefore, in the dialogue now involved in presenting the Gospel, the knowledge of other faiths opened up in recent years will be of great help. In fact the Christian evangelists who helped in opening them up did so because they believed that such knowledge would be helpful.

w.s.c.—4

The basic pattern of a dialogue remains the same; but at every stage a knowledge of the other person's background is of great help.

In a dialogue one starts with an agreement. In his speeches to the Jews, St Paul starts with God's covenant with Israel and his promise of a Messiah; in his speech to the Athenians he starts with the common religious quest of man. When Paulinus in ancient Britain preached before King Edwin and his chiefs, he evidently started with the common human concern about future life. Our knowledge of the religious context of the other party in the dialogue will teach us where exactly the agreement should be based; but it always has to be a quest common to both parties.

But to stop with that initial agreement is to eliminate dialogue and live in the illusion that there are no disagreements. Disagreements do exist; and hence the need for dialogue. Disagreements must be faced, and the greater the knowledge of other faiths, the greater the knowledge of what these disagreements really are. Our disagreement with the position of Islam differs from our disagreement with a Hindu Advaitin; and our disagreement with an Advaitin from that with a Hindu theist. We may find that our agreements with a Hindu theist or a Muslim will be the basis of our disagreement with the Buddhist.

But to stop at disagreements is to lose faith in the possibility of evangelism. The step from the stage of disagreement to that of ultimate agreement is the most important step in a dialogue and the most important act in evangelism; it is to convince the man with views so different from ours that God's offer is being made to him also. Since all men belong to God, and the commission to evangelize is to evangelize all men, that step must be taken. But the step from disagreements to an ultimate agreement must in each case arise out of the particular disagreements we have faced in that case, and therefore cannot be the same in all cases. Sometimes it is an argument that takes the evangelist to the final stage; sometimes it is his character and sincerity; sometimes it is an unexpected event or opportunity. But if the evangelist is himself convinced about the truth and the urgency of his message, he will find God working with him and lifting him to the ultimate stage; for it is he who finally bringeth men unto himself.

MEETING MEN OF OTHER FAITHS

Heinrich Meyer

DURING the past the encounter between Christianity and other religions or ideologies has very often been burdened and falsified by the fact that it was nearly always conducted in an abstract, impersonal and intellectual manner. A Christian 'system of thought' and another 'system of thought' were compared and the two were weighed against one another, God knows according to which standard. Quite apart from the fact that intellectual systematization more often than not is the most inappropriate means for grasping the real essence of a religion, the systems all have changed, particularly in modern Hinduism, Buddhism and Islam and even in the so-called tribal religions. But we have to be even more radical in our criticism: we never do meet a religion or another faith in an abstract form. We encounter men, individuals and groups, adhering to a certain religion, holding a particular faith. Religion always is, even in its most institutionalized form, in reality a very personal, existential matter. I propose therefore to adhere strictly to the subject given to me: *Meeting men*, and thereafter only to consider what happens if these men hold another faith, never leaving out of view the fact that it is first and last man with whom we are concerned.

I

Meeting men always means a most exciting venture, the result of which can never be foreseen. Things happen to both partners of that encounter. We are no longer alone in that self-content or maybe desperate isolation of our own personality. There is another, a third personality, perhaps even many more, all of them as much individual personalities as we want to be.

Such encounter with other men is nearly always influenced by seemingly contradictory discoveries: on the one hand we detect that our partner is very different from us. His language, his features, his attitude, his history—every minute produces additional proof that he differs from us. On the other hand we are urged on to understand our partner and in doing so we realize how very like we are at a deeper or at least a different level: he is a human being, a personality like us. Hunger and satisfaction, joy and sorrow, confidence and distrust move him as much as they set us moving.

This double discovery of difference and likeness in our partner lays open the whole immensely variegated field of human relations, full of dynamics and tension. In this field we move and meet other men. If we try to discover the governing norm and standard of behaviour while we thus move on the field of inter-human relations with its repulsive and attractive forces, we arrive finally at a very simple, very unwarranted and very powerful factor: the governing norm, the decisive standard is my own personality. I am the standard ruling my behaviour towards my fellow man and judging my partner's behaviour.

I like him because he is like me. I distrust him because he is different from me. It may be the other way too: I am attracted by him because he is different from me. I dislike him because he is so very much like me. Whichever way we act and react the fact remains that I myself am the standard of behaviour, the criterion of judgment, the norm according to which my partner is measured.

Now this is certainly unwarranted, yea, ridiculous. This is the last thing which should happen when we go out to meet other men—that we, limited, earth-bound human beings should make ourselves or permit ourselves to be made the decisive criterion and norm for other human beings. Yet this is what happens daily on all levels of human encounter. It has become an almost subconscious habit with us. So much so that even as Christians we succumb to the temptation of making our brand of Christianity, our theological conviction or opinion the unquestioned standard of judgment. Nobody need be surprised, very few indeed are surprised, that we apply the same unwarranted and wholly inapplicable standard naïvely when meeting men of other faiths or of no faith at all. The missionary efforts in the past were not altogether free from this naïve assumption that what *I* am, do, think and say is of course right because I did, I thought, I said and believed it.

II

The very Gospel which we believe and proclaim puts an end to this naïve and—looking upon it with the eyes of other men—overbearing and unbearable attitude. The Gospel says: Jesus is the Lord. He alone sets the standards. He alone is the Judge. He alone has the authority to rule all human behaviour and all interhuman relations. The very questionable authority of man, including myself, is definitely broken and destroyed by the unquestionable Lordship of Christ.

The same Gospel says that I, like all men having usurped an authority which did not belong to me and having defied the authority of him who alone is the Lord, am a sinner against God and men. *I should be broken and destroyed like the false Lordship I had usurped.* But I live. My Lord was broken and killed for me. I live by his grace. I live because he took me into his life. Hence, I, the sinner, do no longer live. I live in him and he lives in me. I am no longer that autonomous, autocratic personality. I am a new man, a true man because true humanity has been restored to me. True humanity means a man reconciled to God, freed from himself, freed for God and God's whole world and all men.

This truth that Jesus of Nazareth alone is the Lord and that I, the sinner, live because of him, and in him alone is anything but a product of my or of any other man's imagination or invention. Nor is it the final outcome of deep and concentrated meditation. I have been overwhelmed by this unimaginable and incredible truth and love. All my fine ideas of justice and holiness, of God's essence and quality are crossed and contradicted by this truth that Jesus, Lord and God, died for me, sinful man, the just for the unjust, the living God for a dead man. I have no option but to trust him against my own judgment and conscience. I have no choice but to stay where I am—in his love and life.

If we do so—stay with him, live in him, trust in him alone—we are destined to meet men. We are in duty bound to go where he went —to meet men. Seeking and meeting men has become our, the Christians', main purpose of life, because it was and is the purpose of his life. Whether men are repelling to us or attractive, whether they like us or dislike us, whether they are friend or foe, kindred or alien, white or black does not matter any more. The field of interhuman relations is no longer a confusing sphere of counteracting influences for us. As far as we are concerned our relations with all human beings are governed by the one simple and clear fact that our Lord Jesus was sent to meet men at their own level and in their own doomed existence—and that we cannot but go after our Lord and with our

Lord to do exactly the same. This holds good for us as individual Christians as well as for the Christian congregations and churches. We are sent because he was sent.

III

One thing is obvious when we set out anew to meet men: we can never again go as people who regard their own knowledge and existence as the standard against which all others are to be measured. We have no reason for boasting of anything we have or are. We are but sinners who marvel every day afresh at the incredible fact that they are permitted to live. The overbearing attitude of knowing better, being better, living a better life is as unchristian as can be. Christianity is neither a superior nor supreme religion, better than any other faith, because our Lord, supreme over all gods and demons, has deigned to become man—like us. The Lord became the slave. Who are we, his slaves, to claim superiority for ourselves?

A second fact is equally clear: if the Lord met man where he was in this world, in flesh and blood, nay more, in man's deepest despair and darkest doom, in the depth of his sin and death, then we have no choice whatsoever of doing anything else. We are not to stand on the safe shore of our salvation and call the others to climb up to us. We are not to remain behind the massive, protective walls of our churches waiting that 'those outside' may eventually happen to find the door or break through the walls. Our Lord expects us to meet man—not where we would like him to be—but where he is in reality.

When we thus proceed to meet men who are different from us and at the same time are similar to us, our first task will not be to judge them, but to understand them. If we want to identify ourselves with them, to talk with them in such a way that there is real communication between us we must know them in that deep sense in which the Bible uses the word 'know' (jāda', ginōskein). To 'know' a man it is not sufficient to describe his personality in intellectual terms. When we come to know a man our heart and soul are engaged as much, if not more, than our head. We shall never know a man and therefore never be able to meet him fully if we are not engaged with our whole existence.

But exactly then when we have abandoned all superiority feelings and when we let ourselves be freed from all temptation to judge our partner we discover in many, many others a difference at the very centre of their personality, in their faith. Certainly we meet Christians too, brethren in the faith with whom we are in full harmony—although meetings between Christians have their difficulties too. We meet others who profess to have no faith at all. It is one of our modern and very urgent problems how we could really meet them. But that must be left to another lecture. We propose to deal here with men of other faiths.

I am convinced that nobody is better equipped to understand adherents of other religions than a Christian. A Christian is—or at least ought to be—free from any prejudice and full of self-effacing love. The World Council of Churches through its Division of World Mission and Evangelism and the member Churches have set up institutes and conduct research-work concerning other non-Christian religions. This is not just a hobby, something we may or may not do. It is an integral part in our efforts to meet men of other faiths, because their faith and religion is an integral part of their life. If anything we should multiply and intensify our study of other religions—never however leaving out the personal dimension. We must and can set the highest standards for our research-work. We can aim at complete objectivity, including all possible approaches for describing and understanding that complex entity, religion or rather religious man—the approach of history and philosophy, of psychology and sociology. We can be watchful against simplification, limitation by a merely intellectual approach, biased interpretation. We can refrain from judging or evaluating other religions. We need not even measure them against our own Christian faith. We have but one task: to meet man and take him as seriously as God has done to us when he became man in Christ Jesus. In all humility we may claim that the evangelical science of religions (*Evangelische Religionskunde*) carried out according to the principles outlined above is the most objective, most sympathetic, most sensitive and therefore most scientific approach also when we try to understand men of other religions.

IV

It is utterly depressing however that using the best method of exploring and understanding the religious concepts, thoughts and practices of other men we come in the end inevitably to the conclusion: they are utterly strange to us. The given problems, the world we live in, mankind and human existence—all are alike to them and to us. But their answers to the problems, their attitude and point of view are entirely different. Maybe we use even the same terminology—but we mean different things by the same terms. All religious concepts and terms are like members, links, parts in a living organism dominated from its own centre. The centre determines and fills the parts. It is at the very centre however that we differ.

We cannot and do not deny that men of other faiths are deeply religious, that they have developed beautiful, lofty ideas, that they do not lack in intensity of worship and ethos. We must readily admit that they take their faith as seriously as we take ours. Even more: in our days we see men of other faiths come to us with outstretched hands pleading with us to join forces. The syncretistic movements all over the world are one of the most powerful challenges to Christianity in our time. If we cannot have unity in terminology and religious practice let us at least tolerate one another and strive after the unity in spirit, in the spirit of religiosity. Non-Christian religions have been influenced by Christian thoughts and terms to a considerable degree and they are ready to consider and accept even more of Christianity.

In spite of all this, the feeling—no, more, the sober knowledge— persists that we are utterly strange to them and they to us. We are divided and there is no human cure for this division. We are divided on the one central issue of our life. We were freed from our old egocentric existence by Christ Jesus, freed to meet other men as persons to be loved, to be served, to be treated as our equals, as our brothers. But they do not know him who has made us free. Our belief in Christ Jesus is at the same time the force driving us to seek and to love other men and the dividing line between them and us.

This is all the more tragic because we know that the people holding another faith are created by God like us. God's mercy nourishes and preserves them as much as us. We know that Christ Jesus died to free them too, that their freedom is at hand, that they too *are* reconciled to God. We know that the living Lord through his spirit seeks them, speaks to them, wishes to evoke faith in them too. When we meet them, serve them, love them we meet and serve Jesus who loves them and is with them. But they do not know it. They do not recognize him who is near to them as much as he is to us. This is the saddening experience we make when meeting men of other faiths: to know that they too are loved by God and might be saved by believing in Christ, and to see that they do not believe.

If we have had this experience there is but one answer. There is no value in attacking their faith and condemning it, quite apart from the fact that we are not called to be their judges here on earth. There is no value either in telling them what we find to be beautiful in their religion, apart again from the fact that we are not called to be examiners of their faith passing notes of praise or disapproval. There is just one possibility left: to tell them as humanly and as humbly, as lovingly and as earnestly as possible about the triune God, their Creator, their Saviour and their Lord—like beggars who tell other beggars where bread can be had freely, like patients, who tell other sick people where they find the right doctor, like ex-convicts who tell other delinquents about the judge who pays the fine himself and lets the delinquent go free. Shame upon us if we the beggars, the patients, the ex-convicts did not speak of Jesus, of nothing but Jesus when meeting men of other faiths and of no faith at all! Shame upon us if we did not do everything, sacrifice everything to win them for Christ, not by force, but by the all-conquering humble love of Jesus.

e. *Mission of the Church in Today's World*

THE MISSION OF THE CHURCH IN AFRICA

Thomas Ekollo

AS is generally known, the work of Christian missions in Africa and certainly in other parts of the world is the result of the great spiritual revival in Europe. That explains why missions were at first the work of Pietists and philanthropists, which has given a good number of African churches today a rather fundamentalist and occasionally a liberal character.

Until the Second World War the true concept of the Church was almost unknown in Africa, and the word 'mission' covered all that the Church stood for. This would still have been no cause for regret, had it only been fully understood that it was a matter of nothing else but the mission of *the Church*. But mission here meant an organization with people coming from outside, with greater power and a more advanced civilization, to speak about God, almost on the same footing as the colonial administration imposed in the name of temporal power.

Throughout this period the Africans showed scarcely any initiative, merely repeating slavishly what the missionaries with their strength and knowledge had taught them. It was the era when to be a Christian and to be civilized were synonymous, when the idea of co-operation between white and black was completely lacking, the white man being the real servant of God and black men were merely his assistants. Two of the most notable features of this time are that missionaries in the same geographical region, no matter how small, each introduced the church practices of his own home country; and that in many cases colonial powers found it hard to tolerate missions from foreign countries. One of the consequences of this is the crushing burden certain missionary societies such as the Paris Mission had to shoulder after the First World War.

The result of such missionary effort, praiseworthy and quite positive in places as we shall show in a moment, is the idea of the Church as something imported, if not imposed, in certain areas.

However, thanks to the intrinsic dynamism of the Gospel, the idea of the 'catholicity' of the Church, continuously germinating in certain souls, did not fail to break through in course of time, giving birth to African Churches in one sense independent of the mother Churches of Europe and America. Thus it is that since the last war independent Churches in Africa, or what are generally called the 'younger Churches', have arisen. The major determining factors in this development, besides spiritual motives, are nationalism and the psychological need to assert one's personality.

The way in which the missions have taken root in Africa is almost the same everywhere: a landing on the coast followed by an advance into the interior, very often along the rivers. In the Cameroun all the earliest missionary stations are on the river banks. And, through a natural predisposition, the coastal tribes are nearly always Animists, the Muhammadans living only in the interior or hinterland. These circumstances have somehow favoured the establishment of missions in Africa, for the Animist tribes of the West Coast in particular have on the whole been quite receptive towards the new religion. Any opposition there may have been at times was only transitory.

Besides their work of evangelism, missions have developed very significant educational and medical work all over Africa. We have not the time to give details of these activities, which are of basic importance in the life of the African Churches.

Since its establishment the Church has had to lead the struggle against paganism, tribalism and numerous customs contrary to the Gospel. Innately religious, the African is a fetishist and believes in spirits. Even as a Christian believer, it is difficult for him to understand the contradiction between fetishism and faith in God, because to him the witch-doctor derives his power from God. Certain marriage customs, such as the bride-price and polygamy, remain stumbling-blocks for him. The roots of tribalism also go too deep to be eradicated at the first contact with the preaching of the Gospel.

After all this hard work (half a century for some missions and more than a century for others), one might ask what results it has produced, or just what binds the Africans to the Church. Now as this is a matter of how the Gospel has made its way, any well-informed person understands the difficulty of making a reckoning here. On the human side you can count a number of positive results, just as others are to be regarded as failures.

Beginning with the credit side, such as it appears, there are reasons for thinking that the message of love in the Gospel has touched men's hearts, as has also the fact that it is a message of power and life. The

African can feel a deep sense of guilt, and the message of the grace of a forgiving God has afforded him great relief. That is why from the beginning those people with a dominating belief in supernatural forces have had to give up their fetishes in order to put their trust in the one God of the Bible. Again, the idea of brotherhood among men has enabled the different tribes to tolerate one another to some degree. One of the tangible proofs of the Gospel as a message of life and power is therefore that the establishment of law and order is made possible.

The same message of the love of God for man, who is made in the image of God, has produced the sense of the dignity of man, and of woman, as well as the equality of the two sexes in the eyes of God. This equality before God has inspired the idea of equality among men and women themselves. Thus men have learned from the concern the Church has equally for them as for women to respect womanhood. There is reason to assume that the Church's insistence on monogamy has had a salutary effect on this change in attitude.

But the most widely felt result is probably to be found in the sense of freedom. Liberated by Christ, we are set free from all things: from sin and slavery as from all oppression. This feeling of the dignity, of the equality of every man before God, and above all of being set free from all things, has contributed without a doubt to the awakening of African nationalism. This is more striking among the Protestants than among the Roman Catholics; hence the Protestant missions, under colonial rule, were often accused of complicity with nationalism.

Among the factors which have contributed to the development of men's thoughts, the Bible is by far the most important. One is surprised to note how the Holy Book which is supposed to provide for devotional needs only has become an inspiration for intellectual thought *par excellence*. This is because the missionaries, loyal to the spirit of the Reformation which would have every man read the Bible in his own tongue, have always tried to translate the Bible into the language of their congregation. Not only has the Bible been translated, but side by side, literature has evolved to help in the understanding of the Bible. Through this translation and with the development of biblical commentaries, the Bible became the best known book, and the concern for its understanding has stimulated a taste for intellectual thought which hardly existed before. And so, unexpectedly, this book has shaped men's minds and refined their culture.

Indeed, the work of the Church has generally brought about many happy changes in men's souls in Africa, but it is still true that the influence of the Church has sometimes been harmful. The most serious thing with which Christian missions are generally reproached is the destruction of certain traditions in Africa just where the originality of its culture in comparison with other races was most marked. But I think that discussion of this would not be of any immediate help. It is more important for us to know what the present position is after so much evangelistic effort.

Here it is most difficult to give an answer. For if there is real progress on one side, to wit: the birth and growth of independent Churches with important congregations, and church leaders who count in the world, there is on the other hand cause for serious anxiety. In certain areas, church attendance has declined considerably; the more advanced people (or the intellectuals) are leaving the Church, the congregations are very inconsistent about the faith they confess, the Church is gaining little ground outside, and the former indifference of non-Christians is being replaced sometimes by direct attacks, etc. In short, the mission of the Church in Africa is passing through a critical time where everything must be thought out afresh.

If we want to try to explain the present difficulties, we should ask ourselves whether the trouble does not arise in part from too easy conversions, for many Africans have adopted Christianity without making a complete break with the past. The requirements of custom and tradition lie deeper than the commandments of the Gospel.

Could the explanation be that the Church's teaching has been too casual, that there has been no proper confrontation between the Gospel and the tradition and real problems of the African? There has been the desire to make him adopt the Christian way of life too quickly, a way which unfortunately in this particular context was after all only the mode of life of the European or the American. From there it is only a step to the equation, Christian equals civilized man. The examples are there; the first is the insistence on monogamy. Without waiting for the African to develop a personal understanding of Christian marriage which could lead to a serious commitment, he has been hurried into the belief that he will be a Christian if officially he has only one wife. And so the distressing conclusion is that it is only necessary to renounce polygamy officially to be a good Christian. With the help of the white man's prestige an ethic was accepted superficially without going any deeper.

The first missionaries were certainly responsible for this situation and their African helpers or colleagues, with little or no instruction, simply aggravated the situation. Instead of instructing their followers about the Gospel they have handed down a dimly understood ethic which they themselves do not really practise. Today, with ideas and real possibilities developing in the wake of Church independence especially, thinking Africans are beginning to subject all that to a severe scrutiny. And few are the faithful who really stand firm in face of the flood of new ideas or merely in the face of all the contingencies of modern life. That is the tragedy of the situation.

The struggle today therefore is not located at the level of ancestral paganism but much more at the level of the paganism of modern man. So we must view evangelism with this two-fold strategy: (1) to win for the Church the millions who do not know Jesus Christ at all; (2) to reinforce the teaching of those nominal Christians whose behaviour does not always reflect their deep convictions.

To obtain the desired results one of the necessary and unfulfilled conditions is certainly the Africanization of the Church. But there is no space to go into that here. In brief we would say that the vague word 'Africanization' means that the work must begin with a recognition of the traditions or cultural values of Africa, and then bring the Gospel face to face with the whole man. That to me seems to be the starting-point for any thorough revision of the teaching programme. And the very first task is to train men and women for work in the Church in accordance with the needs of the day. It is not only urgent that the academic level should be raised, but also pastors must be trained for the necessary meeting between 'Africanity' and the Gospel. Here we must pay tribute to the World Council of Churches, which, as the result of careful consideration, is offering the means to strengthen the theological faculties in Africa.

Another problem of present concern for the Churches in Africa is the presence of the Church in the world and the witness of the laity. At this stage in the construction of the new Africa, all the Churches are conscious of their responsibilities. Gradually people everywhere are studying ways of co-operating with the Governments in cultural, economic and social development schemes. Even in the realm of politics we are giving up the traditional resignation of aloofness; we are more and more convinced that the Church has a message to give in politics and to Governments. The various announcements and public declarations made by the synods on different occasions are witness to this.

After this rapid survey I cannot close without noting the special interest the Churches in Africa attach to ecumenism. And I believe I am not mistaken in claiming that our Churches are ready to bring their contribution to this sphere. Generally speaking, our members are disturbed, horrified, by the division of the Christian Church. They do not tolerate it and await impatiently the unity so much desired. That is why there is no real African reserve towards the ecumenical movement, why the Churches, once they become independent, do not hesitate to apply for membership in the World Council of Churches and everyone is rejoicing over the Second Vatican Council. You can sometimes reproach them with simplemindedness, but what is very sure, they long fervently for the unity of the Church. On the purely African plane during the last fifteen years or so, regional groups have been formed, taking the name of 'federations', 'Christian Councils', and so on. These steps towards union recently took concrete form on a continental scale in the formation at Kampala of the All Africa Conference of Churches.

In conclusion, let us say that the American-European mission has come to a close and has given birth to Christian Churches which will join the Churches of the whole world in sharing God's mission for the world. This mission has these urgent tasks: the witness of the love of God for man-in-the-world; the witness of the Gospel in the face of non-Christian religions, modern paganism and ideologies of every kind; the sense of love for one's neighbour.

In all and for all, to proclaim in the most persuasive manner the sovereignty of Jesus Christ for the reconciliation of man with God and then of man with man, these should be the primary objective, the justification and the mission of the Church in Africa.

INTO A NEW ERA TOGETHER

C. H. Hwang

ON the day that President Kennedy died, seven men were meeting in mid-Formosa to talk of a United Church which one day must come into being. An Anglican bishop, a Lutheran president, a Methodist superintendent, a Presbyterian stated clerk and a Baptist theologian met with two others on that day, when a monstrous act underscored the world's confusion. We had come with expectancy and in spite of the tragic news which had robbed us of strength we left with expectancy and with a greater determination to work together for the vision we had seen together. Our trembling world threatens us and challenges us but God speaks his word through it because only God can shake God's world. What did we seven men talk about? Our conversation was concerned with how the body of Christ might become more visible in Formosa today and tomorrow in spite of the existing sad divisions among the Churches. In practice this meant how could we take joint action in mission at various strategic points, so that we might be obedient to the living Lord of the Church now? It is the matter of obedience to him that is and should be our ultimate concern.

I believe that this concern is very much alive among the Churches in the new Asia of today. We just simply cannot go on with 'Business as Usual' according to the ways which we have inherited. This is not because we are not grateful to our Mother Churches who, to use Paul's phrase, 'begat us in Christ'. Our very existence stands as an undying memorial to their missionary obedience. No, it is not lack of gratitude and appreciation. It is because we are in a *new* situation in Asia, a very revolutionary situation, which is shaking old foundations. The pressure from the world is very strong; still more, the pressure from the living Lord is even stronger. If our Mother Churches had begotten us only in Presbyterianism, in Lutheranism, in Methodism, in Anglicanism, the matter would have been simpler. But they begat us in Christ and his life will not leave us alone. They placed the Bible in our hands and that strange book will not let us alone. The Bible's witness leaves us wondering whether the pressure of the world is simply the pressure of the world alone; might it not be the pressure of him who so loved the world and who was in Christ reconciling the world to himself? In the shaking of the foundations of Asia, of the whole world, we feel more and more called to make some ultimate decision. Again out of obedience to him we are to be found meeting here and there often, like the disciples of old, 'on the evening of that day' (Jn. 20:19, R.S.V.) or as at Pentecost 'together in one place', with plenty of perplexities but also with expectant hope, for the crucified Lord is risen from the dead.

Let me introduce you to one of these meetings. For several weeks my colleagues and I have been meeting to plan the work we are going to do in our Research Centre which the Theological Education Fund has helped us to set up. And I want to share with you our discussions, because they are a window on to the Asia of which we are a part and a microcosm. It is our deep common concern—Presbyterian, Methodist, Episcopalian—how we can serve our Churches constructively so that they may in turn act responsibly and creatively to the new situation emerging in our land. This is a situation which is common to all Asia where in every country the old orders are changing and revolution dominates every aspect of life.

When in 1937 I left our island to study in England it was a colony of Japan. Every country in Asia through which I passed, as far as the Suez Canal, was either a colony or a semi-colony of a Western power. In 1947 I came back via the same route; the situation had changed, and it has been changing rapidly and radically ever since. The so-called colonial era has gone. A new era has come. To achieve independence is one thing; to build a modern nation is another. Nation-building, this is the vortex round which an unprecedented mixture of expectation and frustration revolves in Asia today. This is another of our urgent concerns. How is it to be related to our ultimate concern—obedience to him?

It is in this living context of nation-building that two other burning questions of Asia are being raised. On the material level, there is the urgent question of modernization, industrialization, etc., those realities which are going on under the now familiar name of rapid social change, but these outward events have an inward significance. They are in fact the manifestation of the social revolution which is now going on widely and deeply throughout the whole of Asia. It has been shaking the foundations of the traditional agrarian social structure, of family life and all the human relationship and *mores* built on them. The generations clash. A man's ways seem treason to his father but are repudiated by his son as outmoded conservatism. Political revolution, social revolution, industrial revolution, rising hopes and new despairs, all these struggle round the Asian man and inside him. How is the Church, the first-fruits of the new creation, to be related to this struggle? Is not its task to be in the struggle with a vocation to share the turmoil because only as this turmoil is seen through Christ's eyes and only as Christ is so revealed as its answer, can the Church fulfil its mission and the nations be blessed?

The old faiths and the old cultures are affected paradoxically by the new movements of secularization and nationalism. The acids of modernity have bitten deep into old *mores*. Our religions, always complex, are now caught in cross-currents of decomposition and renewal, sometimes aided and sometimes opposed by new nationalism and other movements. This is of great significance for the Churches in Asia. It is a time when men, consciously or unconsciously, are crying out of the deep and crying out for the depth. It is a time when deep encounters deep. This is a time of opportunity for the Church which cannot be ignored. The Churches in these nations must be drawn into these depths, called there by God that they might rediscover their own depth, find anew their own unshakable foundation. The call is *Ad Fontes*. In this encounter we can only be reaching the living God at the frontier of depth where he is reaching out to us, namely in the decisive event of nation-building, in confrontation with the social revolution and above all in the encounter with the dying and renewing of indigenous cultures and through redemptive wrestling with the non-Christian religions. There is a real danger that we may lose our bearings as we are involved in all these but there is an even greater danger that we may not meet the living Lord if we are unwilling to go 'outside the camp', for it was there that he was crucified and rose again. If we refuse to go outside the wall, we shall become a ghetto, irrelevant and unrelated to Asia today and tomorrow and we shall eventually become a museum piece, a relic left over from the colonial era!

Our depths are known to us in the Bible. This is an Asian book. Preserved and mediated to us by Europe and America it must be reclaimed by Asians in their task of rebuilding. This Bible must speak to a new Asia through Asian commentaries in Asian terms. Its riches must be mined by Asians for a word in season to neo-Confucianism and resurgent Buddhism.

These are some of the things we have talked about in connection with our Research Centre, under four headings of special concern: (1) Biblical exegesis and interpretation, (2) the Gospel and culture, (3) Church and society, (4) mission and unity.

I have been sharing with you these problems of Asia as they were reflected in our joint conversations. But conversation is not enough, it must be accompanied by joint action.

In my own Church we are approaching the first centenary celebration in 1965. It was the challenge of this coming event that, in 1954, caused the Presbyterian Church to launch its movement 'To Double the Church in Ten Years'. We started with 236 congregations on the plains in 1955 and by 1962, *i.e.*, within eight years, 196 more congregations had been added to us, with 40,000 new members. But this is not all. An even more miraculous event took place among our mountain peoples. In 1945 when the war ended, there was not a single church in the mountain areas, where evangelistic work had been forbidden by the Japanese Government for fifty years. Who would have thought that the Church in the mountains would grow by such leaps and bounds so that by the end of 1962 we had 385 congregations, a Christian community of over 70,000—more than one-third the total Aborigine population? Who would have believed these things possible in 1940 when all our missionaries were forced to leave, our seminary closed, and many Christians put in prison? I would not like you to think that such a growth is taking place in all of the new nations in Asia. But what I do want to say is that such a possibility is always with the Church in God's good time. As the Church lives by the power of the Holy Spirit it must be always expectant for a movement of the Holy Spirit to take place. Numerical growth is important, for it is also a sign of the Kingdom. So our Church exults as it moves forward to its centennial year with a goal of 1,000 congregations and two per cent of the population. But is this enough? There is room for thanksgiving but not for complacency. As we draw nearer our set goal we are aware more and more that the world around us has been changing and this change has been more dynamic than the change in the Church. Eight years ago a revolutionary land reform took place in Formosa which has radically changed our rural communities and, more important still, the mentality and expectation of the people living in them. Within these eight years an eighty per cent agricultural island has become a fifty per cent industrial one, with a mass exodus from the rural communities to the cities. New factories appear weekly and with them an ever-growing working class. Eight years ago there were one university and three colleges in Formosa and now there are eight universities and twenty-two colleges as well as 400 secondary schools and over 2,000 primary schools. Are these not the concern of the Churches in Formosa? How are the Churches to be there, where the the people are and where the new frontiers, decisive for the future, are emerging, to penetrate them with the fragrance of Christ? Can we Presbyterians face this alone? We are still less than two per cent of the island's population increase. Ten years ago, there were only Roman Catholics, Presbyterians and two very small denominations in Formosa, but now there are over sixty denominations. Altogether the Christian community is still less than four per cent of the total population. We must not be tied to the thought that we shall always be a small minority nor always live in isolation from each other. To our great joy the arrangements for our centenary are now in the hands of an interdenominational committee, chaired by a Baptist pastor. This is a symbol. Churches which began work in the island ten years ago recognize that their real start was in 1865. Also, it signifies a determination that we shall move into the second century *together*. The problem for us and for all the Asian Churches is the nature of our 'togetherness'. We are convinced that the understanding of our unity and the necessary prelude to its fulfilment is in joint action together, particularly Joint Action for Mission.

I spoke at the beginning of seven church leaders meeting to plan Joint Action for Mission in one island. Much is already being done jointly, more united work is planned for the immediate future and in addition three steps were agreed upon in preparation for our advance into the second century together.

The first step will be a comprehensive study designed to understand the situation of both the Church and society in Formosa.

The second step will be a series of seminars to discuss and analyse the study and then to establish priorities in a programme for joint action.

In 1965, as a third step, the church leaders, having established mutual trust, may invite the secretaries of the related boards to come together for study and jointly to make decisions, set goals, priorities and projects. They might inaugurate a five-year plan or a succession of five-year plans with annual re-evaluations.

Behind this thinking and planning, the underlying conviction is that the Churches in every land must become one authentic missionary community, and grow both extensively and intensively as the community of the first-fruits awaiting the harvests of its Lord. Colonialism is gone but its dual infection lingers in the Churches; we are blighted by Western denominationalism and by a 'beggar mentality' which, accustomed to being the object of missions, hesitates to become the responsible subjects of mission, taking full part in the mission which is Christ's. The home base now is everywhere and as we recognize this in every country the missionary task takes on new perspective. We proclaim a God who loves the world and seeks to reconcile it to himself. This means that we do not stand outside and beckon men's souls only, we stand within our societies. We have our part in the nation-building which everywhere is taking place and we tell of a Christ who saves as well as judges the nations. We stand within our cultures and preach a Gospel which has power to redeem all things. But if the home base is to be everywhere we must revolutionize the relationships which exist between all Churches. The mission is Christ's and therefore the call of the mission comes to all Churches. In this mission, we may not remain in isolation from each other, for *in* him is our common life and *for* him is our common mission. How are we to be bound together in this common task in ways which will ensure its integrity and success? While national and denominational boundaries still exist they cannot be ignored but they must be crossed. As the crossings become more frequent all barriers will be lowered and some will disappear. One day all must disappear. In Asia we rejoice that already there are signs that this is beginning to happen. Over two hundred Asian missionaries have crossed not only national, but confessional boundaries. There are Japanese missionaries in Thailand, Sinhalese in Nigeria, Filipinos in Indonesia and many more. We rejoice, too, that the East Asia Christian Conference is providing for the Churches in Asia in their revolutionary situation, not only fellowship in Christ but also new thinking. At the three situation conferences held at Madras, Amagisanso and Singapore we heard the call for Joint Action for Mission.

As an authentic missionary community emerges in every nation across the six continents, as ecumenical relations draw all the Churches closer and closer into one body for the one essential mission of Christ in and for one world, we see the new rôle and image of the missionary. I see them linking all the Churches: men and women who have crossed national and confessional and cultural boundaries. I see every Church sending them and every Church receiving them—a company of Christ's dedicated slaves and apostles, captives in Christ's triumphal procession, spreading everywhere the knowledge of him who makes all things new.

I see this company of missionaries not only as a symbol of the one united Church, but also as a sign and instrument of a new world which is one and undivided, in which the boundaries have been removed, new nations thrive and prosper without bitterness and nationalism has given place to concern for each other and for the whole world.

The centenary of a young Church in a new society under revolutionary changes is but a sign and a pointer to a new era which is far greater. Atomic power and space exploration are the latest footnotes to God's command that man shall have dominion over nature and subdue it, but they also point to man's existential predicament— namely that he is doomed without God. To the community which knows that 'God was in Christ, reconciling the world to himself', this new era is nevertheless of God and comes to us with apocalyptic signs that herald a *kairos*. To meet it with trembling for the ark of God, fears for our ecclesiastical institutions and demands for our denominational rights and prestige—this is unthinkable. Rather let us meet it with a vision of the new heaven and the new earth, of the new humanity and the new world. So do we pray, 'Come Creator Spirit, enable us to go forward together into this new era which Thou art opening before us'.

THE NEW SHAPE OF CHRISTIAN MISSION IN THE UNITED STATES

Robert W. Spike

WHEN I was first asked to be the bearer of this report on missionary opportunities and challenges in the United States, a year ago, there immediately formed in my mind the kind of speech it would be. It was a speech I had made in essence many times before. But this is not that speech. A year has altered the dynamics of the North American scene in a drastic way. The claims of Christ upon that scene are now being felt in a new way.

And what is the difference that a year has brought? A year ago we were a nation blinded still by our apparent success. I do not mean that we were a people without anxiety and conflict of all kinds. Everyone knows that is not true. We were troubled by our international responsibilities. The meaning of the Cuban revolution confused us. Racial strife was a continuing shame. But over all the impress of a successful, affluent nation busily intent on creating a new technological society was dominant.

The fact of our growing urbanism fascinated and worried us. Our population was mobile; it had increasing leisure time; it felt estranged from any roots in the earth or in a community of generations. We seemed to be a people whose greatest problems were blandness and lack of passion. And this was what seemed to be the target of Christian mission. How could the Gospel be proclaimed with power to a satisfied people? We concentrated on the inadequacy of our missionary structures. There seemed to be a great deal wrong with our parish system and our old missionary institutions, so heavily weighted in favour of nineteenth century society. The real centres of people's lives were no longer confined to their residential communities. Because of the speed of transportation and communications, everyone lived in a mass society, in a sense every member of the nation in instantaneous communication with every other. And at the same time, parts of people's lives were increasingly hidden from others. The Church was big and powerful, but it was carefully segregated from every other part of life. Its job was to keep alive the nostalgic memories of other times. Its job was to feed the personal emotions.

What concerned Christian missionaries most then was how to break out of the iron grip of this increasingly rigid technological society, and to preach Christ as Lord of the whole thing. We needed new songs of the Lord in this strange land. We needed a new living language of Christian faith. We needed new outposts of teaching and preaching and healing in an affluent society. And to this we were giving our attention.

Then in the providence of God, there erupted into clear view what had been there all the time, but we had not seen it for what it was. It is the humanitarian revolution in the form of the Negro freedom movement. It certainly is not a new thing in our country. Racial discrimination has been the deepest chasm in our national life since the beginning. And for the past decade, the new leadership of the Negro people has been moving the twenty million black men who are American citizens towards the full realization of that citizenship. And it was not that Christian Churches were not aware of the sin and shame of segregation. We had all passed high-sounding proclamations about racial equality in our church meetings. We had missionary study units on race relations. We, White Americans that is, felt vaguely guilty, but also convinced that slow progress was being made.

Then last spring began a series of events that shocked us into the awareness of how wrong we had been. The desperation of black people in many parts of the country reached new depths. They moved into street demonstrations at great personal sacrifice and potential danger. Hundreds went to jail in Birmingham. Up to date over 50,000 people have been arrested for civil rights demonstrations of one kind or another in this year. We have been through a series of violent deaths from Medgar Evers to our own beloved President that has shaken us to the core. Suddenly our image of who we are as a people seems very different. These past six months have been times of deep changes in the psychology of the whole country. I do not mean that suddenly everyone has lost their prejudice, or even that genuine repentance has come upon us. In many places, the resistance to integration has hardened. But what is happening is that for the first time long-buried feelings are thrusting their way to the surface. One of our novelists[1] some time ago wrote an important book called *The Invisible Man*,

[1] Ralph Ellison.

describing the black man in the North American scene. The black man is no longer invisible. He is seen and known, and all at once he stands like Nathan with his finger against the chest of the White American and says, 'You are the man'. Thousands of White Americans are for the first time feeling that finger and looking around in confusion for someone else to blame. But suddenly there is no one behind them. We are in the midst of a serious inventory of a society that has used many means to keep the Negro invisible—quasi-legal means in some parts of the country, but in all parts of the land subtle social and genteel means to deprive him of full acceptance into the main stream of our life.

For the first time, industry and Government recognize the potential disaster that can come to the whole nation if we do not change our ways. You cannot keep one tenth of a people segregated in a mass society which depends for its existence upon consensus and mobility without destroying the society.

And to our great shame, the Church is very late in awakening to what it must do. It is to our shame because we have seen so clearly for a long time the evil of racial segregation, but we have been unwilling to use our power to make any effective changes. The great new fact about North American Protestantism and Orthodoxy this year is its willingness to use its secular power in the American scene to achieve integration. The Commission on Religion and Race established by the National Council of Churches in June is a token of that new commitment. It was chartered to move into the midst of the struggle, to engage in demonstrations, to take risks, to do anything necessary to try to bring justice to our injured fellow citizens. This we have done, aided and supported at every hand by all of our major communions, and by the leaders of those communions. We work closely with all the major civil rights groups. We work closely with Government. We are the single most effective group working to secure the passage of the vital civil rights legislation now pending before the Congress. We are working toward the elimination of every last vestige of discrimination practices in our church life, from parishes to church institutions. This new ministry has taken us into many places where tension is high, and sometimes into trouble with local police in the South. We have encountered the blunt presence of Nazism in Mississippi, where an heretical doctrine of white supremacy invades State government, the mobs and sometimes even the Churches.

The most heartening thing is that this bold venture on the part of the governing board of the National Council of Churches has been confirmed by the action of the General Assembly of the Council meeting last week in Philadelphia. That body made up of representatives from all over the country took actions that were hard-hitting and specific, far beyond any of our expectations. The Churches are now at least partially involved in the struggle, and for once on the right side.

But what of the larger meaning of these events that have so convulsed our nation? It is as if the mask of self-delusion had been removed. We have to face what we ought to have known was always present beneath the veneer of generosity and gregarious goodwill. We see ourselves in our darker side, selfish, grasping, suspicious and are shocked by the capacity for violence.

Beyond a new confrontation with our own sinfulness, however, there is something else. That is the growing awareness of the existence of the same revolutionary discontent at the base of our society that exists in nearly every part of the world. It is fed by the terrible injustices that white people have visited on darker people the world over. It is fanned by the vast economic discrepancies between the top and the bottom levels of a nation's life. It is, perhaps, the age-old cry of human misery, but now amplified and instrumented in a technological society.

It is the human protest against the machine and a drive on the part of the lowly to mount the machine and help steer it rather than to have to dodge its relentless progression. But what is new for citizens of the United States is that this mood, this movement is a real part of our common life.

What Negro Americans have known for a long time, many White Americans are just now learning. To be honest, many still have not comprehended that we are in the early stages of a profound social revolution in our country. This past summer and fall I have seen at first hand what it is like to live under tyranny—to be harassed by local police for encouraging people to vote, to be followed and to have your phones tapped. This happens in only a small part of the country, but it is a cancer that infects the whole nation.

The Christian mission in such a time is clear—to proclaim the righteous will of the just and loving God, to enter into the struggle on the side of justice, to bring healing and reconciliation between estranged peoples. The actual shapes that this ministry take will be varied. They include active entrance into the political arena to get just laws. At the moment this phase of the struggle is focused on legislation that will extend federal jurisdiction into areas the states have formerly held sovereign. We have a formidable task in trying to convince church people that active work in support of this legislation is an essential act of stewardship. Our historic fears about mixing church and state are now being more realistically assessed in the light of Christ's kingship.

Another kind of ministry is one proposal for the delta area of the State of Mississippi. This is the hard-core area as far as segregation is concerned. Here are the last vestiges of the old feudal plantation system. Civil and social rights for Negroes are effectively denied because the right to vote, the right to education and the right to work are controlled by a few white families. Here the most militant of our protest groups have dug in, and in the face of much persecution are making progress in voter registration. Here the Division of Home Missions of the National Council of Churches in the U.S.A. and a number of its constituent boards plan to establish greatly needed ministries of literacy training, community services and perhaps some forms of economic redevelopment—in effect, to put into operation the kind of mission programme that is so useful in under-developed societies all over the world. Our home mission agencies have a long history of similar services in other parts of our nation—among migrant agricultural workers, in city slums, among American Indians. Never, however, have we projected a ministry that was so likely to be resisted by local political and economic power. Anything that is designed to aid the Negro in his fight for full equality will be violently opposed in Mississippi. It is a dangerous mission.

And this is why mission forces need help from our brethren in other lands. The awareness of what it means to be a missionary in a revolutionary situation is coming to us late. We need the help of mission workers who have experience in ministries of education and healing in hostile environments. We need the support of the prayers and offerings of churches from every corner of the earth. The oneness of the mission has never before been more apparent to many of us. The fate of every man is bound up with the fate of Christians in the United States, black and white, as they struggle to achieve a truly free society.

It is not only in Mississippi that this ministry must be refined and sharpened. In the great northern cities, perhaps the most bitter struggles will finally be waged. Complicated economic forces keep moving white and Negro apart—in the communities in which they live, and the places where they work. We need help here as well. While I am at these meetings, I hope to have the opportunity to discuss the possibility of such help with those of you from other parts of the world.

I began by saying that until very recently much of our attention in mission circles has been focused on new forms of ministry appropriate to our advanced technological culture.

The urgency of our new struggle—how shameful it is to use that word in this connection—does not negate the significance of that concern. The two motifs cross one another like interacting arcs on a graph. The new age and the new-old struggle for full humanity in full interchange provide the setting for our ministry.

Here we must practise our Christian faith. Here we must live in faith using every bit of imagination and courage which God can give to us. It is not so much a question of making the Church relevant to this powerful vortex of forces into which Christ has led us. It is not so much trying to outguess or outwit the secular forces that are now interacting in our country. No one need sit down and write a new theology. What is required is an eruption of Christian courage, commensurate with our abundance of grace which has been so undeservedly poured out upon us. Pray for us.

MEETING THE INTELLIGENTSIA

Kathleen Bliss

'THE intelligentsia' does not mean, as I understand it, the same as 'the intellectuals', who are what the Americans call the egg-heads—the people with brains who teach in universities and carry out research and write books and contribute to learned journals and so on. The intelligentsia are the creative minority in the making of culture. I suppose it is not possible to be a member of the intelligentsia without brains, but it is certainly impossible to be called part of the intelligentsia with nothing *but* brains. Sensitivity of a higher order is needed, and creative imagination. Who belongs to this creative minority? Not all artists, musicians, writers, but those who form public taste and who are followed by other lesser men in their own fields: not every scientist, philosopher or economist, but those whose ideas are new today and become part of what is commonplace tomorrow. Difficult to distinguish from the intelligentsia and perhaps part of it are the people who create little themselves, but have a sensitive understanding of what is new and important. Some of the great critics and patrons of the arts, the publishers of the unpopular book which becomes a force in the following generation, perhaps also the high-powered broadcasting commentator and the rare educator.

One of the essential marks of the intelligentsia is that they are, in a sense, a collectivity: they explore beyond their own fields and make that exploration the inspiration of their work. Their intercommunication overleaps national cultures and political barriers; somehow or other their work in widely separated fields expresses the spirit of an age.

There is also something else to be said about the intelligentsia: they are, in their own fields, craftsmen. It is useless to have a supremely perceptive eye and ear or a leaping imagination alone. Nothing can be conveyed except by the disciplined use of tools and materials. To fashion words, cut stone, draw an architect's plan, shape a symphony, formulate a scientific theory, *all* need a craftsman's skill and experience based on endless practice to gain mastery, control, precision. The materials of the physical world have to become the means of expression for the intelligentsia as for the common man in common tasks.

Technology and the Intelligentsia

What do we think of the technologist in this discussion? The rôle to which he is commonly assigned in the public view is that of putting into production the ideas of the scientist. But technology certainly owes its origin also to craftsmanship. The wheel, the lever, the pump, the spindle, the pulley, the oar, the rudder—all these and many other inventions designed to help man in the early stages of his long battle for dominion over nature were in use long before the scientific revolution and are still in use today. I spent a day last month in a technical college which turns out, among other technologists, aeronautical engineers. They were still using for students an old very much home-made wind chamber on which one of the teachers of the school many years ago, whose name was Handley Page, carried out the experiments which led to the development of aero engines associated with his name. The technologist sets to work to tackle a particular problem and he makes an aqueduct or a suspension bridge if he is a civil engineer, or scientific fibre or a detergent if he is a chemist; if he is a chemist, he uses physical tools, and more and more mental tools such as mathematical formulae for his work. A peculiar kind of snobbery elevates pure science and despises technology, and even fastens on the technologist the quite unwarranted label of being *the* secular man! This is an unpardonable attitude for Christians to take up, if they do, whose Lord was a carpenter. The technologist shares in the shaping of our present world not only by devising the mass production processes of industry, the drugs of medicine, the fertilizers of agriculture and so on. He also has his representatives among the creative minorities who form the intelligentsia.

Secular Faith

The process of secularization has, among other things, abstracted one area of life after another from any overt dependence on a metaphysic or on religious perceptions of meaning and purpose, and set them going on processes of their own which gather momentum. There are among the intelligentsia many who whole-heartedly welcome this process and hope to see it carried to the point of the total disappearance of religion from the human scene. No one expressed this point of view more powerfully than the German philosopher, Nietzsche. It is not on the pathetic faith of the Christians that we should make our attack, he said, but upon their stultifying ethic which dwarfs and imprisons man and prevents him from realizing his great potentialities by making him afraid. Nietzsche's ideas found expression in the music of Wagner who brought out of the mythological past the gods of German tribalism and clothed them in glorious music. Nietzsche's superman which was meant to be a great secular humanism, a glorification of man, was taken by the Nazis and turned to the bitter use of annihilating men for the glorification of the superman of Nazi dreams. But Nietzsche's ideas are not dead: they form part of the intellectual background of at least some types of secular humanism.

I do not know why Christians allow this word 'humanist' to be used so easily and so exclusively by people who are not Christians. After all, the people who first called themselves humanists were Christians like Erasmus, interested in the study of the products of the human spirit in arts and sciences. Do we care about these human achievements? We should not give in too easily to using this name to describe those who call themselves humanists and explicitly deny all religious belief. So I will call them 'secular humanists'. The intelligentsia are the descendants both of the great Christian humane tradition that glorified God in the arts, philosophy and sciences, and also of those who were the children of the Enlightenment. These two traditions have changed, intermingled and reacted upon one another. But if one were to take only the short view one would have to say that in certain fields of creative activity the leading figures are men who have rejected faith. If wishing to call themselves anything, they would say they were 'humanists'.

If we complain that metaphysical thinking has gone into eclipse as a result of the analytical work of linguistic philosophies, then so has atheism. As the Roman Catholic writer, de Lubac, pointed out, the atheist of today is not the metaphysical atheist asserting a position: he is the *practical* atheist. Many secular humanists are atheists in this sense: they take their stand on a practical decision to rule the God-no-God issue out of order, not on the agenda. They argue, as Nietzsche did, that only when man fully renounces all reliance on divine providence or grace, all obligations to a built-in notion of a moral law, can he shoulder the burden of making his own destiny by his own powers. This is not, they say, either *hubris* or negativism:

... unbelief without any effort to help shoulder the consequences for mankind is not humanism ...

Unlimited shared responsibility for creating the conditions for all of a life worthy to be called human, a human providence, is the colossal undertaking to be shouldered by man without God. Men face together the common problems of mankind, the classical evils of ignorance, poverty, and disease, the spectre of insecurity, the characteristic weaknesses of human beings, the population nightmare; on their side they have the arts and sciences and the vast resources of social co-operation ...

Without some response to this call, without voluntary enlistment in the human enterprise, without something of a Promethean spirit, there is no humanism worth speaking about, for humanism is more a passion than an intellectual position.[1]

The task of humanism is indeed a Promethean task, especially if to these ethical demands are added that intellectual task of equally Promethean magnitude, as it is perceived by some humanists. Karl Popper,[2] for example, speaks of the human task of bringing rationality and order into a world that is not rational: science and social planning are for him as for many other humanists the means to this end.

The humanist appeal, in spite of its crudities, has great attractions, especially in our universities and among many people of intelligence and goodwill. It offers an encouragement to corporate action against the world's suffering; a way of leaving on one side as unanswerable the searching questions of man's being and destiny. It is a way out, but not an easy way out: it makes serious-minded converts, not least from among Christians in despair about the question of truth in Christian faith. In a sense humanists have it all their own way: they combine devotion to the ideal of intellectual openness with a passionate commitment to men's deliverance from hunger, poverty, ignorance and disease. This makes a creed without an orthodoxy and without a church. What would happen to humanism in a world from which all visible forms of Christianity had disappeared? Can a passionate devotion to social causes exist indefinitely with intellectual openness,

[1] H. J. Blackham: 'Humanism: The Subject of the Objections', introductory essay to *Objections to Humanism*, ed. by H. J. Blackham, Constable (London, 1963), pp. 27–8.
[2] Karl Popper, *The Open Society and its Enemies*, Routledge and Kegan Paul (1945–7).

and tolerance? Is the humanist not open to the possibility that he will become passionately concerned to feed the hungry *by whatever means*, that is to say that he is opening the way to handing over men to the processes of technology?

God: Not on the Agenda

There are extraordinary by-products of a decision to leave the God-issue altogether out of account. For example, I was present at the Berlin meeting of the Congress for Cultural Freedom four years ago, which contained among its members a representative cross-section of the 'intelligentsia' of the world. As soon as Christianity was mentioned it simply could not be ignored; every kind of attack was launched, but in a way that made a member of the Congress say to me afterwards, 'None of these people would dare to give to any other subject the triviality of consideration that they think is good enough for religion.' The captiousness and ill-temper manifest that phenomenon of the practical atheist—that he still has to blame God for not being, and, lacking the lamb of God who truly carries away the sins of the world, he resurrects the Old Testament scapegoat and ties on its back his curses on the Church and sends it shambling off into the wilderness.

Another by-product of a decision to leave the God-issue alone is that it sometimes has the effect of making it equally impossible to place the man-issue. The possibilities of the human figure in the visual arts become exhausted and only abstraction remains. There does not seem to be the hoped-for release into the 'genuinely human' by the abolition of God.

The purposive planning of the mediaeval village, or the township of the English Georgian or American colonial period, or even of the small industrial community of the first industrial revolution has no modern counterparts; our planners plan for parts of life, for men's lives have fallen apart.

I do not think that it is just a Christian illusion to think that as religion has been removed from the whole of life into a department, so all the other departments have fallen apart. Prophetic voices, which are not all Christian voices, speak of the danger to man of this situation. Who has expressed it so urgently or in such sombre tones as Lewis Mumford? Are not the secular existentialists in their way saying the same thing when, for example, Jean-Paul Sartre says there is no such thing any more as a human nature? For him 'Man' had disappeared and we are left with the category of the absurd. Camus, too, saw the same estrangement of man in what are really religious terms. The concept of man's alienation from himself and from the world may be Marxist in origin but it is a theme explored by all, and our modern secular prophets owe as much to Kierkegaard as to Marx. The picture of a loss of wholeness, a restlessness endlessly searching for human relationships that will satisfy more than the animal passions, is a true picture of much of life in the secularized civilization of our day. The young live in their own pop culture created round this theme.

Rebuilding a Religious Dimension in the Whole of Life

I cannot believe that the mission of the Church is really to invite men to take up religion as a department of their lives. We have to invite them, along with ourselves, to a rebuilding of this religious dimension in the whole of life on new terms. The old terms were largely dictated in their form by man's inadequate knowledge of nature and his slender powers over it. The new terms have to be within our new knowledge, within our new powers, within our new relationships in new societies.

What sort of points of mission can we see? Perhaps I may name three. The first is the quality of human relationships. It is for the Christian to show that he knows what friendship is by being a friend; knows what the depths of human polarity in sex mean as a dimension of all life by manifesting it; rethinks and relives the fading relationships of the family in terms which are consistent with our new social patterns but make the best and not the worst of them.

Whether people are outside or inside the fellowship of a Christian community the problem is basically the same—that of putting the humus into the soil of human relationships—giving them the richness and depth that come from openness to divine grace. This cannot be done just by personal witness. Christians have to be working in the field of social planning and political decision to turn back the forces that sell out the person in human relationships to the onward drive of technological advance which, left to itself, cannot do other than enslave man.

Secondly, to many people in a secularized society Christianity still means human service or first presents itself to them as such. Many men and women experience the impersonality of social provision and the impossibility for social provision to keep pace with changing needs. The old, whose vastly increased numbers in our midst are a direct result of the scientific and technological advances of our time, gratefully accept such service. The young, in large numbers and in unexpected ways, feel and express the urge to give service. Technology produces a vast new category of needy persons—the redundant whose skills are made obsolete. A spirit made sensitive by Christ seeks to know the need and find the means of meeting it: the quickened conscience is a part of meeting it.

Thirdly, we can take *au pied de la lettre* the statement of St Paul that when we eat the bread and drink the cup that are the body and blood of the Lord, we *proclaim* the Lord's death. Our worship is not just an auxiliary aid to Christian living and service: they are in fact our preparation for worship. Worship is the centre of our life as a Christian community and we are called to make it as worthy an offering as sinful men can offer. We have no idea how widely what is done in worship and for worship does in fact spread.

We should not be afraid of the fact that the Church is looked at by the sociologist as part of his material and that books describing the life of a parish will be reviewed in sociological journals, and books on pastoralia will be discussed in journals of social work or psychotherapy. If we have educational insights of value, they will appear in professional educational journals. New versions of the Bible, developments in liturgy, in church music and architecture, all form part of the wide observation and voracious reading of at least some part of the various professional *élites* that make up the intelligentsia. It is unforgivable in us that we should tolerate the shoddy.

The work of the intelligentsia springs out of common life: both the subject matter and the tools have this source. What really speaks to the non-Christian is the voice of the Christian who is in his own realm of discourse. But the Christian member of the intelligentsia is fed by those things I have just mentioned—the whole tradition and life of the Church. I spoke earlier in this paper of the influence of Nietzsche. The chief translator of Nietzsche's work into English, once said, 'If one speaks of the influence of Nietzsche then what should be set against it is the voice of Dostoevski.' This voice came out of the heart of Russia, speaking with immense power of the tragic depth and glory of the human condition. That voice echoes still in Russia today and while he is read there *is* a mission among the intelligentsia. Out of Russia too has come perhaps the only truly great Christian novel of our century, *Dr Zhivago*. Boris Pasternak, half Jew, half Christian, pours into this novel a quality of compassion for human persons caught in the agonies of revolution and war which fulfils his own design, which was to write of the human scene lit by a radiance coming from beyond it. Thus he interprets in his own way, in an age of unbelief, the essential Christian theme that man is only man at all as he is man before God.

You will think, and rightly, that I have been looking at this matter from a rather exclusively Western point of view. Some of the problems are universal. The relation of the *élites* of science and technology to the rest of those who make a culture is bound to become a worldwide problem. Different types of scientific method are applicable to every aspect of culture. What would we know of the development of any culture without scientific methods applied to archaeology, history, the study of ancient texts and so on? Science and technology, that is to say, not only create new things in culture but assist in the discovery of the old. No creative minorities can work without some reference to what has gone before. One of the most powerful forces in nationalism is that it combines an appeal to tradition with an openness to new forces. New nations are looking to their universities to be the places where the rediscovery of the old and the development of the new are fostered on behalf of all the nation. Unfortunately, Christianity often has the appearance of not caring for either, of holding men back from participation either in the enjoyment of the past or in the making of the new. Any member of the intelligentsia who accepts this may become a Christian but will cease to be part of the intelligentsia. A crying need of the Church in new nations is to listen to its own young. Among them are, somewhere, members of the intelligentsia of tomorrow. Dare I—perhaps I can, as being myself among the elderly—quote the saying of Pascual Jordan, the great physicist: 'Old men do not accept new ideas; the young grow up into them.'

THE GOSPEL AND THE INTELLECTUAL WORLD

Mauricio A. López

IN taking up the matter of the intellectuals we must confess to a two-fold limitation: the limitations of space and our almost exclusive reference to the Western situation with which we are a little more familiar. Who are the intellectuals? Their heterogeneity as a group makes it difficult to characterize them. The word 'intellectual' has a whole group of apparently disparate meanings. To make things more complicated, it once described a person, and now is a person; an adjective has become a noun. Boborykin, a little-known Russian writer, was the first to use the word 'intelligentsia' in the last century to designate a certain type of cultured people—professors out of work, disenfranchized priests, nobles who had lost their position, artists in constant hunger—a group that was involved in inflammatory criticism of the Russian society of that time and was also proposing the establishment of a more just and rational order for society. These people—the 'humbled and offended' of which Dostoevski speaks—were all influenced by German romanticism and idealism.

Although the situation of the intellectuals is not everywhere the same and has been somewhat modified today, it is possible to note certain traits which this group still has. Their principal traits are three: cultivation of the intellect, inclination to and love for culture, and the desire to influence public opinion. The intellectual works with ideas, notions, thoughts. He divides up reality but then on reflection organizes it again according to the dictates of his intelligence. He is a witness who with boldness and imagination can penetrate the secrets of the universe, the depths of the soul, the complexities of society, and gain a clearer and more coherent understanding of these realities. Camus said in his *Chroniques Algériennes* that his task was to expound the nature of things in order to de-intoxicate the spirit.

The realm of concern of the intellectual is the life and works of human culture. Among intellectuals may be discerned a creative nucleus, such as the scientists, philosophers, theologians, and artists; a transmitting nucleus constituted principally by professors, and the various performing artists; and an executive nucleus as is the case of

the engineers, doctors, lawyers and economists. No doubt this break-
down is a logical scheme which is often not borne out in practice,
since there are intellectuals who move from one sphere to another.
Intelligence is employed by them as a dagger of political and social
agitation. Thus Socrates believed himself to be invested by God with
the mission of being a stimulant, or maintaining the people awake,
just as the gad-fly does not give the horse a moment's rest. Unamuno
called himself a 'lay apostle' tramping the roads of Spain as a pedlar
with a huge bag full of truths for the people. Intelligence exerts
influence on society, contributes to the moulding of character and to
the opening of new perspectives. The intellectuals do not themselves
make supersonic aircraft nor develop penicillin nor cultivate the rose
with their own hands, but rather give to us the fundamental insights
which in turn enable us to fly faster than sound, cure a galloping
pneumonia, see new beauty in the flower. Whitehead indicates that
the often appalling practical results of ideas are more decisive than the
greatest victories won on the battlefield. In this sense the influence of
Hegel, for example, felt by both the right and the left, is greater than
the influence of Napoleon; no one today questions the fact that Hegel
is one of the most powerful forces in the changes we see in the world
today.

I. *The Intelligentsia in the History of Thought*

The intellectual was already known in the Graeco-Roman world.
His was an aristocratic group which transmitted its knowledge and
culture individually, with the purpose of forming spiritual traits.
With the creation of universities in the thirteenth century the situation
of the intellectual changed. It was now no longer a case of individual
instruction but a real community where professors and students
gathered to teach and be taught. The intellectual now became a
distinct category in the Middle Ages, with a touch of rebellion that
came principally from the students. Knowledge and culture were
organized according to functions in society; and thus served to produce
doctors, canon lawyers, theologians and jurists. This universe of
knowledge was crowned by theology, because everything that was
learned ought to aid a person in his path to God. The Church is the
guardian of spiritual and cultural life. The same intellectual life in
the main ran through all the universities created by the ecclesiastical

hierarchy. An episode with comic aspects gives us a glimpse into the situation of the intellectual in all periods. Abélard, an exemplary case of the professor of his day, wants to marry, but his sweetheart, Héloïse, disarms him with a good dose of common sense. 'You would be unable to give yourself equally to wife and philosophy,' she said, in order to remind him immediately of the incompatibility of the life of the scholar and the household, of books and the cradle. The wealthy could do it. They lived in palaces where they could find a quiet refuge apart, where also they would not be 'crucified by material pre-occu-pations'.

In the fifteenth century the Renaissance produced a new cultural influence that is profoundly linked with a progressive secularization of society. Man, who has until now been considered a prisoner of the mediaeval system of thought, begins to be emancipated and to discover the humanistic culture as such, with its own values that are independent of Christian values. Man now no longer sees himself as a child but as one growing up, able to weigh reality in its own terms. Truth now is not a divine gift but a search by means of the twin tools of reason and experiment. All understanding, all knowledge must be measured by these two yardsticks. A fundamental event, the invention of printing, contributed to the wide diffusion of this new way of feeling and thinking. With the book the intellectual now had his own device which was capable of spreading his ideas and his view of things to a larger and larger audience.

It was inevitable, the conflict between the culture nourished by faith and the culture sustained by reason. The theologian felt obliged to react against the scientist, the believer and the unbeliever went off on separate paths, and faith and reason diverged. It is a conflict which is uniquely Western and has arrived in other parts of the world only by importation, and which is illustrated strikingly in the case of Galileo. It has continued throughout the whole modern period, as is illustrated by the apprehensions about Darwinian evolution and about the new historical methodology which Renan and Strauss applied to the sacred texts. It would be timely to ask if the extraordinary development of the sciences of man in recent years will not encounter the same failure to comprehend on the part of the Church. That would be to prolong a state of affairs which in the last analysis presents a false choice between faith and reason. We say false because it disregards human reality and its true situation in the world.

In our time we are beginning to see clearly the Promethean dimension of man. The industrial revolution transforms a rural civilization into an urban civilization; the creative power of man increasingly alienates him from his natural environment and puts him in a situation dominated by technology and organization. In this sense capitalism and socialism do not differ greatly in results, since both in the last analysis propose to establish a functional society, rationally structured. Marxist prophecy is optimistic about the unfolding of all this. Marx predicts, in his *Notes for the Holy Family*, that socialistic humanism will secure the reign of liberty, will put an end to the quarrel between nature and man and the enmity of man with man. Liberty and necessity, objectivity and self-affirmation no longer will be contradictory terms. The whole concept of the development of human history is bathed in this good fortune of the regeneration of man by man. It is the Promethean affirmation which is behind Bertrand Russell's saying that even though God may have created the universe this is no obstacle to our recreating it.

If Marx were alive his optimism would be more cautious. Man runs the constant risk of alienating himself in his work, and of objectifying himself and dehumanizing himself in his rôle as producer and consumer. In this light there is incumbent upon intellectuals the vitally important task of putting into action a humanism which respects the human condition. We must be grateful to God that in a universe which tends to become self-contained, the voices of the poets are again heard.

There are many trends of thought which mould today's intelligentsia. A summary judgment would place Marxism as one of the greatest influences of our times and undoubtedly the actual ideological spur of the social revolution in process. Existentialism—a true reflection of the contemporary crisis—is still alive in its reaction favouring the inwardness of the individual, the exaltation of freedom, and a somewhat spiritualistic personalism. Scientism is less pretentious in its aspirations and abstains from building great explanatory theories; except for this, Marxism has taken over, more intelligently, scientism's valid premises. There are, also, several oriental systems, like yoga, 'tantrism', Zen, anthroposophic movements, which promise a better education of the intellectual and spiritual forces of man without having to go through a Church or a particular confession. The Christian intelligentsia also counts in the world of thought; nevertheless it does not seem to establish such general or strong trends as Marxism, for example. The Christian intellectuals believe that the Gospel is not a developed ideology, a type of philosophy, a system of ideas coherently organized to explain the world and life. This does not mean that they have not provided a Christian interpretation of work, matter, man, society and history. A significant contribution has been made by some Christian thinkers of all confessions, who have tried to re-establish a communal personalism using the valuable perceptions of Marxism and existentialism and encouraging a new dialectic between the person and the community that avoids the extremes of individualism and collectivism.

2. *The Intelligentsia in the Social Environment*

Saint-Simon used to refer to the intelligentsia as being 'men of genius' or 'social industrialists', as distinct from other groups made up of workers, peasants, employees and landowners. Despite their being a rather varied and individualistic community, they have a sense of purpose which in a way separates them from the rest of society. This condition has given rise to various forms of anti-intellectual reflections; people accuse them of being cold, of having a complicated intellect and of feeding devious feelings. The redoubtable Jean Cocteau approved of Luther's throwing the inkstand in the face of the devil. The French artist said he deserved it because, after all, 'The devil is an intellectual.' Even without desiring it, the intellectual is a public figure and he plays a prominent rôle in society. He is often considered a prophet who has the gift of calling things by their name, a priest who seeks truth and judges human acts. Mounier considered him the spiritual man who judges everything, but stressed at the same time that his moral authority is not a commodity won forever. It is an authority which in each deed can either dignify or corrupt itself, exalt or degrade itself. His rôle is that of adding to an 'ethic of conviction', a constructive and responsible attitude so that his criticism will not stay at the level of mere negation. To stand for a resounding 'no' to a world of alienation and human need is not to keep such things from existing. That is why his contribution is demanded in the formation of the means to make possible a transformation of such a situation.

What is to be done about poverty, about injustice, about ignorance and disease? Will he remain aloof or will he throw himself fully into the political whirlpool? It would seem that the logical outcome of his protest would be revolutionary action; however, that is not the usual thing. Most of the time intellectuals are content with being the catalytic agents of change, the creators of revolutionary ferment; seldom do they foresee or put to use the means for a radical transformation. The often quoted example of the frustrated political incursion of Plato into Syracuse, repeated at other times with similar results, puts him permanently on guard. There is in the intellectual a kind of reluctance to descend to the level of direct action or to keep track of the meanderings of political life. On this level everything comes out incurably adulterated. As the character Garcia says in the work of Malraux, *L'Espoir*: 'Every form of action is irrevocably Manichean.' It is an agonizing dilemma, this one of escaping from both a Manicheism of action and an angelic purity of conscience. Koestler portrays it strikingly in his book, *The Yogi and the Commissar*. The yogi considers politics something wicked, and that is why the intellectual must give up revolutionary action. The Commissar, who is also an intellectual, is so driven by the eagerness for transformation that he is bent on struggle without turning back.

It is unlikely that there exists an intelligentsia socially disconnected, and in an age in which technology permeates everything and in which the achievements of science have released from nature such unsuspected forces, many are asking if the intellectual should not take a part in the working out of political decisions. The great Italian physicist, Enrico Fermi, whose research in nuclear physics had as its outcome the making of the atom bomb, received on a certain day an invitation to watch the first test on the New Mexico desert. In the face of such an explosion and the immense mushroom of fire that rent the air, he suddenly realized the implications of the application of the 'theoretical space', which he had discovered in the quiet hours in his study. The apocalyptic vision of the explosion left him mentally depressed for months. The mathematical equations inscribed upon the order of human relations posed an alarming threat. Thus the pressing need arises to place theoretical systems within the framework of human life, otherwise every intellectual conquest, every ideological system is likely to become a menace to itself. It is perhaps this dangerous juncture of history which is moving the intellectuals of different ideological bents to seek for an international dialogue. Contributions to this are the remarkable development of communications, a living in common of historical time, and a certain equality in the spiritual and material standard of life which allows us to live on the same level with one another. Distant cultures have become neighbours, and we are beginning to have the impression that we are marching toward a common humanity.

> Today whites have ceased to see without being seen . . . that privilege has come to an end; black torches light up the world and our white heads are no more than tiny lights swayed by the wind.[1]

UNESCO has made a notable contribution to this internationalization of intellectual life in providing an exchange of ideas and persons. But outside UNESCO, movements are attempting to establish a kind of world-wide policy of culture, linking up dialogue and co-operation among men of different ideologies, thus promoting a coming together among peoples. We hail this event. Communication and mutual understanding are indispensable for the making of this on-going universal civilization, and it is well known that so long as men maintain dialogue, the sword stays in its sheath.

3. *The Gospel Preached to the Intelligentsia*

Today the world is subjected to a profound change in all its structures. The Church lives through this period of time under the patience of God for the purpose of proclaiming Jesus Christ as Lord and Saviour and to minister to men in the varying circumstances in which they live. This historical situation in which we have been destined to live is not intrinsically bad nor absurd: but it is lived by men of flesh and blood and is capable of receiving a new meaning. The changing world situation does not mean that the opportunities for evangelism are increasing or decreasing, but it does mean that the Church finds a challenge to prepare itself to enter into a fertile dialogue with this world.

In the topic with which we are dealing the Church has before it very great opportunities and enormous responsibilities. It seems to us that it is indispensable that we give special consideration to the layman who is primarily occupied in intellectual pursuits, helping him to deepen his faith and to resolve the agonizing dichotomy which so many of them feel between faith and reason, and between faith and

[1] Jean-Paul Sartre, *Situations, III*, Gallimard (1949), p. 230.

their profession. Much is said today of the failure of the *élite* and of an age of 'technocrats' who are more interested in plans and statistics than in the men who have suffered all sorts of alienations. I think that much of the guilt for this situation must be accepted by us Christians who have so largely ceased to think and to live in close relationship with these intellectuals and have been unable to see in Jesus Christ the frame of reference for all human knowledge and values.

The communication of the Gospel to men of high culture must, in the first place, recognize them as men—men like all other men; and they should not be separated from humanity into a special class with prefabricated ideological labels. The intellectual is, above every-thing else, a man who feels, lives, loves and dreams as all other men do, and has a personality which is not defined nor encompassed by any kind of label. We should not decree *a priori* that they are unreach-able or inaccessible; but we must recognize that the Christian shares with them a common road. Pagans walk this road in the name of Marxism, of existentialism, and of science; the Christian must walk this road in the name of the Incarnation. The unbelieving intellectual is actually a necessity for me to understand and grasp intellectually my own faith. When Marx exiled God because his presence distracted man from his own vocation of being man, and asserted that God should be defined as the 'fantastic realization of the human essence', we can do no less than be grateful to him for having obliged us to descend from the plane of essence, however heavenly it may be, to the plane of existence. An essence is devoid of reality and in it we can never be able to distinguish the God who chose to reveal himself in Jesus Christ.

To this effort to approach the intellectual, to understand him, to walk the road with him, we must add the joy of the proclamation of the Gospel. We must speak powerfully of God if we are faithful to our biblical foundations. But the biblical language is strange to our contemporaries; it has crystallized into a jargon which is no longer comprehensible to men of our day. Here we reach a fundamental aspect of our task, because words and dialogue are the true realm of the intellectual. The Christian must speak of Jesus Christ in words that are commonly used in daily life; he must not fear to speak in the language of the secular world as the Apostles did when they utilized the forms of communication of the Graeco-Roman world. The watch-word here is 'faithfulness' to the very heart of the biblical message in order to avoid the distortion or destruction of faith which is communicated through a medium which did not originate in that faith.

To live with men—in this case with the intellectuals—does not mean that we are to remove the rough edges from the Gospel; we must conserve the fact of the Cross, the judgment of God and the grace of God for the sinners, which all of us are. We must remember that the Word of God is as a sharp sword which discerns the intentions of the heart, and that the Cross will always be a scandal for the wisdom of this world. Whether or not the intellectual is converted is a question which only God can answer. I would like to recall here what Karl Barth said to a German pastor—what matters is to know God is not against them—and this is what we must believe for them.

Let us proclaim the Gospel, but let us not forget the service which the Christian intellectual should contribute to every cultural enterprise. We should not think that the Christian intellectual is provided with some kind of infused wisdom or some dogmatic formula straight from heaven which will solve all the problems of life. It is part of our testimony to work with the intellectual in the task of discovery, of experimentation and of broadening the horizons of human knowledge. Faith does not impose any kind of epistemological limitation, but it does provide us with an inescapable ethical reference. The Christian must realize that all is possible but not all is valuable; that his life is determined, not by what he discovers, but by his dependence on Jesus Christ. It is the task of the Christian intellectual to demonstrate to our contemporaries that faith is the deepest expression of the values which guide the searching and concerns of modern man. Paul Ricoeur, when speaking of liberty which is a precious value for man, asks himself whether liberty can really be respected and exercised with responsibility unless one believes that the human creature is made in the image of God and that his destiny was bought with the price of the Cross.

The Christian will accompany the non-Christian along the path of life, he will be with him, and will share with him his hopes for a society with a more equitable distribution of wealth, more human concerns and in which culture will not be the privilege of the few. He will point out that there are certain analogies between the Kingdom of God and human society, and that because of them, it is worthwhile to struggle for justice and for a peaceful life together for men. At the same time, he should help him to be open to the course of history and will point out that the best organization of human society does not necessarily bring peace to human hearts, nor reconciliation of man to man, that every cultural labour is precarious, relative and never final, and that it is necessary to be alert to avoid imprisonment within ideological absolutes. He will point out the complexity of the fabric of history, he will herald the new advent of Prometheus, the maturity of the secularized man, the eagerness for progress, and he will raise a word of warning lest we fall victim to the secular illusion of the self-deification of man.

4. *Latin American Epilogue*

The members of this conference will surely have realized as they have walked along the streets of this very remarkable city, that there is a sharp contrast in the level of life and culture of the people. With certain minor differences, all of Latin America is this way: an immense Janus with two faces which must be contemplated with close attention in order to discern its multiple facets. What has happened here? There is a four hundred year old explanation which can be told rapidly. The Spaniards came in search of an unrealistic Utopia: the creation of a society on the model of declining Spain, proud in her loneliness and an enemy of everything that was modern. The men who came to our land were imbued with a tired and expended ideology. Hegel, at a later date, was to say that Latin America lived outside history and was pure nature. At the beginning of the last century, our peoples became independent nations. Our liberal leaders dedicated themselves to the task of building our national life, using as models France, England and the United States, which were then the most advanced countries. They were men who longed for the full, modern life and they depended on the nations that postulated the ideals of democracy, freedom and progress. Nevertheless, this was a struggle which exceeded their resources: the conservative interests allied themselves with those very nations who were at that time in a period of imperial expansion; and as a result the wings of the young republics were clipped and an economic and social régime was perpetuated until our own times when it is dying a slow death. The result of this circumstance has led the soul and culture of Latin America to oscillate between the call of the already petrified indigenous culture and a nostalgia for European ideals as an example for life and action.

Gonzalo Castillo has referred to our social revolution, which is still difficult to define because its course cannot yet be discerned. To date, it has been an affirmative sign that a people has abandoned its passivity and that it desires to enjoy the dignity and well-being to which it has a right; a responsible nationalist affirmation that endeavours to launch itself into the path of progress without necessarily closing itself to foreign contacts; an attack at the very foundations of the structures which have brought the economic deficiencies and the social injustice which we suffer. This social movement is a formidable challenge to the intelligentsia of Latin America which until now has been polarized by liberal and Marxist ideologies. This social effervescence has led the intellectuals to look deeply at our own reality which embraces all of the national life. It is to be hoped that this new conscience among the intellectuals will help them to sift the watchwords which come from Washington and Moscow, and enable them to enter into an open dialogue without prejudices and for the benefit of our countries. It is also the duty of our intelligentsia to approach the people, to forge a new Utopia, a new humanism which is respectful of social justice and personal dignity.

The social revolution presents a serious challenge to the Christian Church. The revolutionary initiative has not been born of the Christian Church, but, while originating in 'Christian' territory, was not inspired by that faith. In any event, we believe that it is a healthful challenge—the means which the Lord has chosen to compel the Church not only to awaken and see clearly the new order which is developing, but also to re-examine her own structures, her mode of life, of action and of her presence in the Latin American world. Catholics and Protestants have an enormous task before them; they are both in the same boat and the two, leaving behind them their antagonisms and resentments, must learn together how to be witnesses of Jesus Christ in our countries. The Lord desires that the mission effect this reconciliation between the Churches, and between the Churches and the people, whom we ought to love and serve with the best of our intelligence and all of our heart.

Section I

THE WITNESS OF CHRISTIANS TO MEN OF OTHER FAITHS

The Motive for Witness

THE motive for Christian witness to men of other faiths emerges with sharp clarity from the biblical record. This has been made very clear by the Bible study sessions preceding the meetings of the Sections each day. Key words such as creation, covenant, reconciliation, and witness have been studied with care. To every Christian and to the whole body of Christ, the mighty acts of God as recorded in the Scriptures are a binding and impelling summons to witness.

These great themes all reveal the purposes of God towards his total creation, together with the joyous response which the Holy Spirit evokes from man. In all of creation God has given to man in particular the capacity of responding to love. It is man to whom God has bound himself in covenant relation. His purpose is no less than the reconciliation of an alienated world to himself in Christ. The Christian, therefore, must be bold to appeal to all men to respond to what has been done for them and to claim all things for Christ. The Christian mission is the proclamation of this message to the whole world: be ye reconciled to God.

Everyone who has experienced the liberating power of Christ is claimed by God to declare his wonderful deeds, in witness to other men. Our proclamation of the Gospel to men of all faiths, or to men of no faith at all, is itself a part of the mighty acts of God. Witness is, therefore, a clear and compelling obligation upon every Christian, every congregation, and the whole Body of Christ.

Our Attitude towards Men of Other Faiths

The Christian attitude towards men of other faiths is basically one of love for all men, respect for sincerity wherever found, and patience to search for ways to bear effective witness. Christian witness to men of other faiths involves more than a simple declaration of Christian Truth, to be accepted or rejected by them. It is important to recognize that a follower of another religion has his reasons for believing in it. These reasons may be part of the preparation for his understanding of the Gospel. It is important, also, to recognize that many followers of other faiths today find satisfaction and inspiration in the ways their faiths are being reinterpreted to lend added meaning to individual, social and national life. The vitality or lack of it that any man finds in his faith, and the sincerity of his search for God, may in the providence of God become opportunities for Christian witness.

The man of another faith offers by his faith—or even by his bitter opposition—a very vital challenge to the Christian. This requires of the witness a searching of soul and a more humble and persuasive testimony by word and deed. The Christian is under the burden, first and foremost, to witness to another man of whatever faith to what God has done in Christ for all men, knowing that God is already at work in that man's heart. Even though in the deepest sense it is God who through his Holy Spirit leads man to decision, yet every act of witness should be an invitation to Christian discipleship.

In the world of other faiths there are some who are secret believers, avoiding for various reasons membership in the visible Body of Christ. There are others who have been influenced by Christian truth, but short of the point of belief. In relation to such men Christians have a continuing and delicate responsibility. In the providence of God, such men may be used by him to work within their own communities of faith. Nevertheless, to be a Christian necessarily involves being brought by Christ into the visible, witnessing community of faith.

There are important aspects of the witness to men of other faiths which are not only individual. They include the use of mass media of communication, provision of Christian literature, participation in the world of scholarly study of the faiths of mankind, the evidence of the collective influence of a faith upon its corresponding culture, and the ways in which one faith as a whole comes into contact with another faith as a whole, in the interplay of human affairs around the world. The Christian and the Christian Church must be ever watchful for opportunities to enhance the witness of the total Christian community to the other communities of the world.

What has been said holds good also in the case of the Jewish people though they are related together with the Church in the history of the people of God. As we believe that Christ is both the fulfilment of the covenant and the light of the world, we must be willing to listen to what the Jew has to say to us in his interpretation of the covenant, but also to bear unmistakable witness to Christ as the Way, the Truth, and the Life, as we would to the followers of any other faith than our own. At the same time, Christians have a vital obligation to fight against any form of anti-Semitism, just as they have a vital obligation to fight against every form of persecution or discrimination as being contrary to the Gospel.

The Christian witness to men of other faiths also calls today for vigilance against religious relativism and syncretism. These may take various forms, such as the mixing of beliefs and practices, slow absorption into other religious systems, the loss of conviction as to the finality of Jesus Christ, and the sophistication that likes to feel itself at home in every variety of belief. Behind all these forms lies the presumption that it is the wisdom of man that establishes the truth.

The Nature of Dialogue

True dialogue with a man of another faith requires a concern both for the Gospel and for the other man. Without the first, dialogue becomes a pleasant conversation. Without the second, it becomes irrelevant, unconvincing or arrogant.

While the basic need of all men, including Christians, is for the Gospel in all its fullness, the individually felt need of any man under his particular circumstances at any given moment also requires sympathetic and informed understanding on the part of the man who will speak to him of the Gospel. Dialogue requires a transparent willingness to listen to what the other is saying and to recognize whatever truth be in it.

In the dialogue with a man of another faith, however, we must be aware that he as an individual cannot be separated from the religion and community which dominates him in all his thoughts and deeds. A dialogue cannot therefore be carried on without a thorough confrontation with his full religious system.

Sincerity is basic. This includes humble acceptance of one's own faults and the willingness to accept the challenge of the Gospel to one's own life—though the Christian witness, too, lives every day only by the grace which forgives sins.

In all true dialogue it is necessary to remember that words and doctrines have deep sentimental associations and emotional overtones for the speaker which they probably do not have for the hearer. Particularly when ideas are to be translated not only from one language to another but from one religious context to another, dialogue calls for a delicate sensitivity on both sides.

From all this it is clear that while there is but one Gospel, and all men are one in their need of reconciliation, the actual circumstances under which one meets a man of another faith are so varied in their significance for the establishment of true dialogue that the effort to approach all men of other faiths under the single category of 'non-Christian', and to prescribe a single approach to them all, is an ineffective beginning to what is, ultimately, a single witness. This variety of circumstances is the more obvious when one thinks of the witness of the Christian to the followers of tribal religions, to secularized man or to the man who declares himself an atheist.

Whatever the circumstances may be, our intention in every human dialogue should be to be involved in the dialogue of God with men, and to move our partner and ourself to listen to what God in Christ reveals to us, and to answer him.

The Call to Witness

Modern means of transport and communication increasingly produce a meeting of cultures in every land, while a growing global technological civilization facilitates a common meeting between men of different faiths. Christians will more and more meet Hindus, Buddhists and Muslims in the countries of the West, and Christians in both East and West will be subject to growing pressures from the ancient religions which are now becoming also world missionary faiths. Whether the Christian Churches would wish this or not, God in his providence is leading Christians in every walk of life in every land into encounter with men and women of other faiths. An adequate understanding of the responsibility and the opportunity which this contemporary situation creates needs to be imparted to the members of our Churches.

The way in which most Christians bear their witness will not be that of the theologian or professional missionary. The more natural and spontaneous witness can be, the better. A great responsibility, however, rests upon our Churches in these circumstances to help all their members to welcome, instead of fear or avoid, contacts with men of other faiths.

As has always been the case, the chief witness of the 'ordinary' Christian man or woman will be borne by loving service and care for persons as persons, no matter what their race or creed. Lives must conform to the Gospel, and deeds are a vital part of witness. Yet witness requires equally to be borne by word of mouth—and it is here that guidance may be specially needed.

From what has already been said, it will be realized that the Christian's fundamental approach to a man of another faith must be the recognition that, for him, Christ has already broken down every barrier. He meets his fellow man as a brother for whom Christ has already died. He will welcome every common interest and every common concern through which he can enter into real fellowship, living his life as a concerned participant in the community of which he is a part. As opportunity offers, he will speak frankly as a Christian, while making it evident that he expects and desires his friend to speak equally frankly from the standpoint of his particular faith. He will seek to be as open to his friend as he wants the other to be undefensive with him. He will listen in order to understand. His object will be to witness to the Christ of whom he is certain, to share the experience which Christ has brought to him, and to invite the other into discipleship, recognizing, however, that conversion is the work of the Holy Spirit.

It must be recognized that although the Christian himself may welcome dialogue and fellowship of this kind, the first approach of others to him may not be of this nature. There are good historical and psychological reasons why the man of another religion may meet him with criticism or attack. This will be the Christian's great opportunity. He must seek in humility to understand and accept whatever truth there may be in the indictment. His witness need not be a defence of Christianity as it is; it should lie in the presentation of Christ and of the essential meaning of the Gospel.

What we have said here about dialogue should also characterize the spirit of the public preaching of the Gospel which will continue to be an essential part of the Church's witness.

Faithfulness to this task of witness to men of other faiths will assuredly increase the Christian's own understanding of the Gospel and devotion to his Saviour.

APPENDIX

Some Remarks Made in the Course of the Discussion

'Too many "dialogues" are in fact double monologues. It is not enough even to listen. We must give evidence of willingness really to hear what the other man is saying.'

'In the process of sharing our concerns with one of another faith we may come to a deeper faith ourselves, and reformulate our Christian doctrine accordingly.'

'Our concern is not to communicate certain doctrines, but to help each man, of whatever faith, to meet the living Christ for himself.'

'We can no longer proclaim the Gospel in our terms and leave it to a man to accept or reject. We must enter into the agony of communication.'

'Do not let us become more technical in our use of biblical terms than the Bible itself.'

'Points of contact are not points of equality, but points of beginning of dialogue. They are determined spontaneously on the spot, not theoretically in advance.'

'There are men in non-Christian faiths who in personal life transcend the statement of their creeds. We, therefore, must not prejudge any man's position by his formal creed alone.'

'What we need is a new *apologia*, using the terminology of other religions, to make clear the new truth in Jesus Christ.'

'Only Jesus Christ makes it possible for me to meet a man of another race or another religion *as a brother.*'

'There is nothing more repulsive in the twentieth century than cultural provincialism. Many missionaries fail because they love people but they do not like them!'

'Let us grasp the meaning of the whole world as having been reconciled. Christians must be much bolder in claiming all things for God.'

Section II

THE WITNESS OF CHRISTIANS
TO MEN IN THE SECULAR WORLD

Introduction

THE title of this section demonstrates one of the difficulties of the subject. 'Secular' means 'worldly'; what then is a 'worldly world'? But in spite of this oddity we knew that those who had assigned us our task had in mind a real situation or series of situations and not an invented one.

For better or worse we did not try to define the various uses of the word 'secular' and its derivatives. We looked at situations as we knew them, and at ourselves, concerned with the Church's mission in the world, and caught up in a process of secularization which has many aspects and which in its main lines is irreversible. Our Bible study spoke directly to our subject: in our Section meetings the time was always too short for all we had to share. We may not be able to put down on paper what we experienced, but every one of us had our understanding of our secular world deepened and our Christian faith illuminated in ways we shall not forget and may be able to share.

We are neither optimistic nor pessimistic about this process of secularization as such. It should not be judged simply by the criterion of what it does to the Church. We mean it when we say that secularization opens up possibilities of new freedom and of new enslavement for men. We have no doubt that it is creating a world in which it is easy to forget God, to give up all traditional religious practices, and at the same time to lose all sense of meaning and purpose in life. Yet we are overwhelmingly convinced that it is not the mission of the Church to look for the dark side and to offer the Gospel as an antidote to disillusionment. We believe that at this moment our Churches need encouragement to get into the struggle far more than they need to be primed with warnings. It simply does not do for us to talk about the problems of affluence, of too much leisure, and so on, to those whose backs are breaking under loads we have never had to bear. We therefore want our words to be urgent, even at the risk of appearing to be one-sided.

We believe that our own Churches in many situations have been secularized in a bad sense; that is to say that they have become a compartment of life, apart from the rest, and have very often submitted to making the best of this. We believe that the time has come for them as institutions to go and join their laity where they are, *inside* the secular world. We believe that our Bible study showed us that 'what cannot be assumed cannot be redeemed'; that as our Lord took on our flesh, so he calls his Church to take on the secular world. This is easy to say and sacrificial to do.

The Process of Secularization

Secularization appears as the revolutionary attempt of man to become emancipated from all forms of dependency. It is occurring in different forms and at different speeds in various countries of the world. In this dynamic situation the destiny of man is in the balance between greater freedom and new enslavement. Will he choose the emancipation which is in accord with the teaching of the Old Testament prophets and of Jesus in the Sermon at Nazareth, or the rebellion against his Maker which can only destroy his life? As Christians we are involved with all mankind in the process of secularization and with the making of these choices which present themselves not once but again and again.

To understand our Christian mission at this time we have to try to understand the secular world. The following are the subjects around which our discussion revolved:

1. Men exercise an increasing control over nature by science and technology. Why call this secularization? Because it has brought men hopes in this world, many of which can be increasingly realized. We are probably still only near the beginning of man's acquisition of knowledge which multiplies at breakneck speed. In our Bible study we saw a number of things about this aspect of secularization:

a. Man's dominion over nature is God's intended purpose. Why then have Christians apparently so many hesitations? Can we not see God's mighty acts in what is happening in our day? Yes, but there is still an ambiguity. Man has learned to rule nature but he has done so partly by submitting to have nature's knowledge on nature's terms. There is no moral purpose in nature, or in the knowledge we gain from it.

b. Any religion that is an attempt to control nature by pleasing nature's gods has no future. The Christian doctrine of creation is quite other than these. The writers who began to express it in the Old Testament were men who already knew God in human history. The world is spiritual because God made it. But there is widespread a debased religiosity which divides the sacred and the secular in a way that is opposed to the Christian doctrine of creation. The process of secularization helps us to see that the material world is God's creation, the place where he calls men to play their part in his continuing work.

c. Dispossessed peoples and nations are awakening everywhere to demand a share in the fruits of the dominion over nature which so far have been the exclusive and arrogantly flaunted possessions of certain nations and privileged groups. Secularization puts into men's grasp the ideological and technological arms to win their aspirations. This new dynamic is overruling past supremacies and exploitations. In humility, man can overcome the inequities of the past through a mutual sharing of the fruits of the control of nature.

2. Secularization also means man's control of his social environment and of his own life. This control is exercised through knowledge of nature and of society. It is idle to underestimate the extent to which men can do this. Out of nature man has created a sort of 'second nature', a world of communities, institutions and techniques by which men live and on which they are far more obviously dependent for their life than they are on nature.

The process of secularization is breaking open the historical limitations of race, class, nationality, and occupation. Men are becoming free from old social stratifications and therefore in principle each man is freed to make his unique contribution. Each man is made by God in his image, with infinite possibilities for using his freedom to fulfil God's will.

In our day men are struggling for liberation from tyrannies of unjust social orders. They are self consciously attempting to re-order society in such a way as to provide for greater human fulfilment for individuals and for communities.

Secular structures have a God-given function to serve men by bringing them into new relationships for production, or education or the exercise of political power. Structures deny their purpose when they become self-serving or when they reduce men to objects or functions. New powers in the hands of men and vast organizations in which to exercise them open new opportunities both for service and for exploitation of men. Both are happening in our world. The fight for justice to individuals and minorities is not over and Christians need to join with all who are prepared to engage in it.

Technological development of communication and transportation has brought men from all parts of the world into intimate relationship with one another. Modern technological warfare has forced men in all parts of the world into interdependence for their very existence. These secular developments remind us that God has created his world for one destiny. This new understanding of our world-wide interdependence calls the Church to a greater ecumenical responsibility.

These last four paragraphs speak of four areas in which men are seeking new ways of fulfilment. It is a characteristic of the processes of secularization that the departments of life, which have had a certain harmony between each other in a religious view of life, fall apart and each develops on its own. This is why so many men feel the weight of unfulfilment and meaninglessness. Reconciliation of men to God and men must in our day include not only persons but also institutions and national and international life. This reconciliation is part of the work of God in which he calls us to take part. It may mean Christian witness in and to the power structures; it may mean revolutionary protest; it may mean active endeavour to make a political structure which does not place man either under the centralized power of the state or between the competing groups of a pluralistic society but creates as yet unrealized forms of community; it may mean patient suffering. Whatever our situation, God is at work. Whatever our possibilities, there will always be a cross. Whatever our success, there will be God's testing of every system. Whatever our failure, there will be his mercy and our undying hope in him.

The Task of Mission

But what is the form and content of the salvation which Christ offers men in the secular world? We at Mexico City were not able to do more than touch the border of this subject. What we have begun to see is not yet a coherent vision, but there are some insights which point in the direction we must go. Christian witness participates in the common agony and hope which men experience in the process of secularization. It should articulate questions and answers from within the modern world and take up the points of decision which God himself has provided through secularization. Thus we can come to deeper understanding of the presence of Jesus Christ in the world and communicate the Gospel.

The pattern of Christian mission in the secular world must therefore be one of constant encounter with the real needs of our age. Its form must be that of dialogue using contemporary language and modes of thought, learning from the scientific and sociological categories, and meeting people in their own situations.

The Christian message to man in the secular world is not only the proclamation of a transcendent God who reigns as the Lord of nature, but also the proclamation of God as the Lord of world history, who became a man in Christ. His divinity has become visible in his true humanity, as he emptied himself to be one of us so that men might fulfil the tasks to which they were ordained in creation.

The Christian message to man in a secular world is not only to be expressed in terms of a religious inwardness which calls men out of this world. It must be expressed in terms of relations here and now, as restoration of man's total relationships, as the making whole of the person in Christ, the new man, who reconciles men in one and the same act to each other, and to God. He is the gracious God in being our gracious neighbour.

The Christian message to men is not only concerned with individuals but also with the Kingdom of God as the destiny of mankind as a whole. The Christian message liberates us for service to our neighbours. Being released from a selfish life, we can use the gifts of God which he has given to us in the process of secularization so that we do not victimize ourselves and others. Technical skills, scientific knowledge, the time of leisure and the power structures receive their meaning in the service of others.

The Christian message to men in the secular world does not call them into exclusive minorities, but to be the 'first-fruits', those who live a life of witness and service for the total community, thus forming the nucleus of the household of God in each land and among every group of people.

This concept of mission in the secular world has many immediate implications, as for example a fuller participation of the laity in world mission (as indicated in the report of the section on witness in New Delhi, but still needing to be spelled out). This new world demands greater ecumenical involvement on the part of the Churches. Other questions, such as the true meaning and form of worship in a secular situation, remain quite open, and will require further study and experimental action. If we take the situation of man in a secular world seriously, and understand that mission has to take place from *within this world*, our church structures including our missionary structures will need to undergo radical change. If we do not submit to God's loving hand we will surely receive his judgment. For the Church is to be the bearer of hope to the world, and is entrusted by God with this gift for the sake of the world.

Meeting here in Mexico in the season of Advent we look with longing for the coming of him who makes all things new.

Section III

THE WITNESS OF THE CONGREGATION IN ITS NEIGHBOURHOOD

Neighbourhood

'NEIGHBOURHOOD'—those near us, who therefore have a claim upon us—must be defined today not simply in terms of residence. In our mobile world, lives impinge upon each other in an increasing variety of 'worlds'. Thus, for example, in modern cities and suburbs our lives often are intertwined less with those who reside near us than with those who are 'given' to us in other communities such as work, or recreation or politics.

The variety and mobility of these increasingly important non-residential neighbourhoods give new dimensions to the task of Christian witness. It suggests the need for new forms of congregation. It underlines the need to discover the essential unity of the mission of the Church in relation to the mobile variety of modern communities. It daily makes more absurd our denominational divisions which cut across the unity men are given in these natural communities.

Witness

In all ages the Church is called to be the sign of God's purpose for his whole creation. This unchanging calling in the changing world is expressed in the Eucharist in which the redemption of the whole world given in Jesus Christ is offered continually for and to the world. Thus if the Eucharist is the sign of God's redeeming work, its redeeming reality needs to be manifested within the broken world of contemporary neighbourhood. Thus when Negro, Puerto Rican, Anglo-Saxon share the Eucharist together in a store-front church in East Harlem, the true secular significance of the event becomes clear. It is a sign of the power of Christ to make 'one new man' from the broken humanity of our world.

The emphasis has rightly been placed upon the evidence of Christ's redeeming power in the contrast between the life of the world and the lives of Christians in their separate communities. The need to witness to the renewing power of God's love as it is shown forth in the community of God's people is a calling of which we need a constant reminder. But it should not blind us to the fact that the evidence of changed lives is often to be found in other areas than a recognized congregation.

(Some members of the Commission could not accept this sentence and proposed the following alternative: 'But it should not blind us to the fact that God is at work also in the activities of secular agencies.'

The discussion raised a theological issue which remained unresolved. Debate returned again and again to the relationship between God's action in and through the Church and everything God is doing in the world apparently independently of the Christian community. Can a distinction be drawn between God's providential action and God's redeeming action? If the restoration and reconciliation of human life is being achieved by the action of God through secular agencies, what is the place and significance of faith? If the Church is to be wholly involved in the world and its history, what is the true nature of its separateness? We were able to state thesis and antithesis in this debate, but we could not see our way through to the truth we feel lies beyond this dialectic. Yet we believe that all attempts to adapt the structures or the thinking of the Church to match the great changes that are taking place in the world will be doomed to paralysis until we can find the way through to a truer understanding of the relation between the world and the Church in the purpose of God.)

Drunkards are reformed in Alcoholics Anonymous; lives broken by fear and anxiety find healing in a group-therapy session in a hospital; homes torn apart by jealousies and conflict find new unity at a marriage counselling agency; families almost dehumanized by overcrowded tenements are restored to better human relationships by a city council's imaginative rehousing scheme; young lives stultified by disabilities imposed upon a particular class or race are lifted into dignity by social and political reform. This should be to us a source of joy and a reminder that the concern of the Church is not only for those things which it does as a separate community but also for the whole of God's work in the world.

This reminder that Christ Jesus, the head of the Church, is the loving and ever present Lord over all the world, gives a new emphasis to the witnessing task of the Church. It reminds us that we are to

watch for the signs of Christ's presence in the communities of the
world. Therefore the Church should seek for the gift to interpret
what is happening now in the events of world history, on the basis of
God's particular work in the history of the events recorded in the
Bible. We are called: (a) constantly to ask where God is at work in the
world; (b) to take the Incarnation seriously: to be 'Christ to our neighbour' (Luther), by serving and suffering through involvement in the
arenas of the world's struggles not only as individuals but as old and
new forms of congregation; (c) by word and deed to interpret for the
world the Saviourhood as well as the Lordship of Christ in the events
of our time.

Thus we see the significance of Christians from a city church in
Taiwan going out into the police stations, trade unions and government offices, and finding that 'in these encounters they discover a
shape of Christian obedience being written for them by what God is
already actively doing in the structures of the city's life outside the
Church'.

Congregation

The increasing separation of many aspects of modern life from the
residential neighbourhood, where congregations have been formed
for so many centuries, is raising in acute form the question as to what
new concepts of the mission of the congregation and what new
forms of congregation are now needed to witness in the neighbourhoods of modern life. We draw attention to the study on 'The Missionary Structure of the Congregation' and urge the member Churches
to join in the urgent task of discovering the forms of missionary
obedience to which Christ is now calling us.

Because we are the pilgrim people of God moving towards the
new heaven and new earth and seeking both to be and to point to the
signs of Christ's redeeming purpose for his whole creation, it is of
the nature of the Church to be open to those new forms of church
life needed for our witness to the Lordship of Christ within the
changing forms of life in the world. Because the renewing power of
the Holy Spirit is available to the Church we should be ready for the
required changes in the forms of our witnessing life. Because the
Holy Spirit is the giver of repentance and new life, Christians suffering
the natural temptation to cling to past forms of church life when they

have lost their relevance, should be open to the gift of renewal in a way unknown to the world.

We would suggest some of the types of form needed today:

a. 'Cell' groups (perhaps becoming new forms of congregation) meeting in the particular 'neighbourhoods' (sociological communities) such as residential communities, trade unions, political life, business. Only in this way can men hear the Word and experience the fellowship of Christ at the places where their anxieties and hopes are faced and where their important decisions are made. Theological reflection must take place at the points where obedience is required.

b. Congregational forms that transcend these particular realms of social life and witness to the power of Christ to bring forth a new humanity which breaks through the separation of class, culture, concern, that so often characterizes the separate 'neighbourhoods'. So, for example, a congregation based in a segregated suburb in New Jersey (U.S.A.), where all the residents are white middle class, is called to find a form of congregational life that breaks through the separations of race, class and culture.

c. Forms of church life which reach out into the vital streams of contemporary life where the fabric of human existence is being woven. Thus in Latin America the Church is being called to find forms which will enable it to witness to Christ's purpose in the midst of the incredible awakening of the masses to the task of demolition of an evil social order—an awakening that constitutes a marvellous conversion from fatalism to hope, from indolence to revolutionary action and from resignation to rebellion. Again the Church is called to find the forms which will enable the laity to be trained to witness to Christ as they go to other lands for government, or industry, or education and play their part in the emergence of the new world community. These two examples point to the importance of the truths we are beginning to rediscover—that the Church is to equip its people to be God's servants in the world, and that new forms of congregational life are needed for the fulfilment of this calling.

We would also point again to the need for unity in these emerging forms of witness. Perhaps the big breakthrough on the road to unity will come only as our divided congregations together turn from their introverted life and seek to find unity of witness within the secular communities of the world. As we reach out into the unities of the world's life seeking to witness to the Lordship of Christ and his purpose to unite all things in himself, the need for unity in our witness becomes increasingly clear. We therefore urge upon the member Churches the need to explore with haste the possibilities of the programme of 'Joint Action for Mission', asking what it means for them in their situation. We are only beginning to see the implications of the awareness that the mission of the Church is not just to three continents, but to six.

The New Delhi Assembly spoke of the need of the Churches to take 'responsible risk' and to be ready to face the possible death of past forms as we reach out to the true unity that is Christ's will for us. We would affirm the need for 'responsible risk' in reaching out to the congregational forms needed if we are to be true witnesses to Christ in the contemporary world. The 'risk' we are called upon to take can be 'responsible', for we are not left without guidance as we venture out into a future which to us is uncertain. Christ is the Lord of the future, and it is an essential aspect of our witness to him that we should face the need for change without anxiety.

THE WITNESS OF THE CHRISTIAN CHURCH ACROSS NATIONAL AND CONFESSIONAL BOUNDARIES

The Summons of our Lord

THE risen Lord summoned his disciples to be his witnesses unto the end of the earth. The task that confronted them was formidable. Ours is not less formidable, nor is it less urgent.

There are many parts of the world where the Good News has not been told.

There are many sectors of life and culture, in which the Lordship of Christ is not acknowledged.

There are millions all over the world who are estranged from the Christian faith.

Christian witness is not in words alone, but in life. The whole Church is called to bear the witness to the world and to do so as one family in Christ.

This requires the crossing of national and confessional frontiers.

Crossing of Frontiers

The missionary frontier runs around the world. It is the line that separates belief from unbelief, the unseen frontier which cuts across all other frontiers and presents the universal Church with its primary missionary challenge.

Other frontiers exist. The most important of these today are between nations and races, between ideological and cultural groups. Many of these nations are newly independent and are struggling for selfhood and a better way of life than they have known. They are caught between old forces dying and new forces struggling to be born. The Gospel must be preached to men where they actually live. This variety of nations and groupings must be welcomed as a part of God's creation but, because of sin, these frontiers become formidable barriers which must be crossed if the witness of the Church is to be truly universal.

When we cross such natural frontiers to witness to the Gospel, we find that the divisions of Christians into their several traditions and confessions build up other barriers which must somehow be crossed if the world is to heed or even to hear the proclamation of the good news in Jesus Christ. It is true that the varying traditions within the Church are also in a sense a treasury of God's manifold gifts. But denominations and their missionary agencies, because of separation, obscure and blur their witness. The world looks at divided Churches, hears their varying claims and cannot believe that Jesus Christ is redeemer and Prince of Peace. So these frontiers too must be crossed if the one faith is to be preached to one world. A common missionary task for the whole world must be undertaken by all the Churches with their varying resources if the world is to hear the Gospel.

Thanksgiving

We thankfully recognize what God has done through the missionary endeavour of the last two centuries. Whatever its failures, it is a testimony to the universality of Christ; it has been the instrument, under God, of the planting of the Church throughout the world, and it has opened the way in crossing all kinds of frontiers. We also acknowledge with gratitude the pioneering work of such international and interdenominational agencies as Y.M.C.A.'s, Y.W.C.A.'s, the Bible Societies, and the World Student Christian Federation.

The achievement of co-operation in the world mission is notable. In education, medical work and all kinds of humanitarian and religious service, the Churches have learned to work and witness together. Not least in theological education has this co-operation been demonstrated and theological thinking and teaching has become increasingly ecumenical rather than denominational.

We rejoice in the achievements of organic unity of Churches of varying traditions in what were mission fields and the further movement towards such unity, not only where the Churches feel themselves a weak minority but where they have been accustomed to think of themselves as strong and influential.

We rejoice, too, that Christian fellowship is bridging gulfs of social separation and injustice and that the one Church holds Christians in communion across formidable political divisions that otherwise seem almost absolute.

Challenge

Our thankful recognition of what God has done should not blind us to the magnitude of the challenge which confronts us. We are still far from expressing the wholeness and universality of the missionary task and the meaning of our ecumenical calling.

1. To fulfil our missionary obedience and to give concrete expression to the Gospel of reconciliation (2 Cor. 5:11–20) the movement of Christian men and women across both national and confessional frontiers must continue.

2. In this age of revolution and nation-building ways must be found to relate all Churches creatively to each other for the one mission of God in Christ, for the one new world into which all the nations will bring their God-given gifts and glory.

3. There is a growing recognition that there are areas of missionary responsibility in all parts of the world where the traditional approach by members of a single nation, race or denomination is an unworkable anachronism. A church in any part of the world should no longer have to look for help in its local missionary responsibility to a single nation, race or denomination, but should be able to call into partnership in its task both persons and resources from many different directions.

4. Churches which are rich in resources and do not feel the need of missionaries from elsewhere to aid them in their local missionary responsibility should ask themselves whether in reality they are not 'wretched, and miserable, and poor, and blind and naked' and in need of spiritual help from other churches. In seeking such help they may find that they have received from the Lord 'gold refined! in the fire' and have become 'truly rich' (Rev. 3:17, 18).

5. The fresh insights that have come to us regarding the missionary calling of the Church in its local setting and the significance of the Christian vocation in the secular world should not blunt the edge of the challenge of the universality of Church and Gospel. Young Christians should be helped to realize that as servants of the universal Christ they must ask themselves *where in the world* and *in what capacity* God may want them to work as his missionaries.

6. It is not enough merely to cross frontiers physically. God's mission demands total involvement in the life of the Church beyond the

frontier, as members of the one Body. Every such involvement is a source of joy for those who are ready to bear the pain of estrangement. In the providence of God the very handicaps and frustrations of foreignness may be for the furtherance of the Gospel and part of the 'wisdom of God' (1 Cor. 2:7). For every Christian is an 'alien' in this world, while in the household of faith there are 'no more strangers and foreigners'.

Breaking Through

What insights have been given to us in this meeting regarding next steps? With some hesitation on the part of our Orthodox members the following proposals are made:[1]

1. The identification and survey of areas unreached by the Gospel—both geographical and sociological; and the presentation of the needs disclosed to Churches and missions;

2. That Churches, mission boards and missionary societies should be encouraged to prepare plans by which the missionary force will become increasingly international, interracial and interdenominational;

3. In all areas where the old geographical homogeneity of the Churches is breaking down due to mobility of population and increasing urbanization, and especially where united Churches have been formed or are being formed, that the mission boards and societies related to these Churches, at their invitation and in consultation with them, work out new plans for the strengthening of the Church, for the sharing of mission personnel and support, and for moving forward in the unfinished mission task.

4. The extension of the use of international and interdenominational teams for specific tasks in witness in industrial centres, in cities, in universities, in the production of Christian literature, in medical work, etc.

5. The intensification of interconfessional theological training for the ministry, the education of Christian youth and of Christian congregations in the ecumenical missionary task.

Ecumenical experience has revealed that co-operation in action can take place at almost every point. The most intractable frontier is that of structure, ecclesiastical and missionary. The growing recognition

[1] The other members of the section wish here to testify to the substantial contributions to this report made by our Orthodox members.

of the missionary nature of the Church sometimes tends to strengthen confessional frontiers in the world mission. World-wide confessional bodies, denominational Churches and missionary societies have, in some places, helped the achievement of organic union; in some other places their influence has blocked locally desired unions. We would therefore urge Churches and missionary societies to perform their work in relation to the total missionary task and in awareness of the problems of mission in unity.

Further we affirm again our conviction that the effective church leadership in any given nation should be chiefly in the hands of nationals and that missionaries who have come to share in the mission of a Church other than their own must learn to work under the authority of that national leadership.

Until He Comes

We believe that joint action in mission is the next step in obedience, to which we are together called. But we must recognize that it is an interim step. If we are fully obedient to the pressure that the Lord has laid upon us we will be led beyond our continuing division into a sacramentally united fellowship, which will make visible that we are one family in Christ.

We must strive and pray for the restoration of the wholeness of fellowship that can only[1] be received in the Eucharistic feast instituted by our Lord and that wholeness of witness that must be transmitted to the world. A divided Church is not only a scandal; it can become responsible for the death of men's souls.

His will is that we should witness to all men. We call upon Christian men and women everywhere to bear this witness across all the frontiers of our time. By such obedience we shall show to the world that God's kingdom is at hand.

With the Apostle Paul, we believe that it is time for us 'to wake out of sleep, for deliverance is nearer to us now . . .' (Romans 13:11, N.E.B.). New idols are set up for man's worship. Ancient idols, repainted but scarcely disguised, are put forward as having power sufficient for salvation. Within the Churches and in the world the sharp choice between Christ and anti-Christ stands before all men.

[1] We note that the use of the word 'only' in this sentence might be viewed with hesitation by some Churches.

The climax which precedes the final consummation of God's kingdom approaches. Therefore our confession to the risen Christ, whose coming again we eagerly expect, requires of all Christians a united missionary obedience at all frontiers and at every battle-line. *Maranatha*. Lord, come quickly.

A SUMMARY

by

The Editor

THE first responsibility which the constitution of the Commission on World Mission and Evangelism lays on meetings of the Commission is to 'formulate the general lines of policy and programme to be followed by the Division of World Mission and Evangelism'. The main instrument for the discharge of this responsibility at the Mexico meeting of the Commission consisted of five committees, each of which considered one or more elements in the policy and activities of the C.W.M.E. The Committees met for four sessions, and their reports were then discussed, amended and adopted by the Commission in its concluding plenary sessions. The full text of the reports, as adopted by the Commission, may be found in the Minutes of the meeting, which constitute the official record. The following is a summary of them.

Committee 1 was a *Committee of Reference and Finance*. It reviewed the Director's Report and made recommendations on specific points from it. It prepared a 'model' budget, amounting to $245,000 in 1965, which was provisionally approved for the next quinquennium, the final decision on it to be taken by the Divisional Committee or its executive 'in the light of responses received from member bodies'. It noted the 'development of the Programme Fund under the authority of the Divisional Committee' (the approved budget for 1964 amounting to $192,750), and considered it 'an important and valuable development'.

This Committee also reviewed a comprehensive statement on 'The Preparation of Missionaries' drawn up by a consultation on this subject held in Toronto, Canada in August 1963 as part of a world-wide study process, and commended it for study by Churches and missionary agencies, urging acceptance of certain 'principles of action' which it detailed.

Two major matters on this Committee's agenda had been sent to affiliated Councils for special consideration prior to the meeting. The first was the question of the continuance of the Theological Education Fund, inaugurated at the Ghana Assembly of the International Missionary Council (1957–8) with a five-year mandate. An advisory committee had been at work during 1963 and recommended continuance with a new mandate covering other elements in theological training than those with which the Fund has hitherto been concerned, and recommending that the C.W.M.E. seek resources up to a maximum of $4,000,000 over a five-year period. This recommendation was accepted, the Commission stating that it:

> . . . is aware that many Churches and mission boards, including those who have contributed to the Fund, have thereby been involved, and will continue to be involved, in additional expenditure in the area of theological education. The Commission is confident that the policy of increased expenditure will be readily accepted, since the development and heightening of standards of theological education constitutes a priority in our time.

The second was a proposal, originating from a consultation on Christian literature at Bethel bei Bielefeld, Germany, in October 1962, and examined by an exploratory committee during 1963, that a Christian Literature Fund should be established on lines analogous to the Theological Education Fund. This proposal was approved. The Fund, administered by an international committee is to be used:

> . . . to assist projects and programmes developed by Christian literature agencies for which they and their supporting bodies accept full responsibility and which (a) give promise of achievement superior in quality and effectiveness to what already exists; (b) are assured by responsible agencies of a reasonable measure of local support; and (c) will be either fully supported without aid from the Fund after a reasonable period not exceeding five years or brought to a fruitful completion within the same period.

One 'guiding principle' is that:

> approximately one-fourth of the Fund should be devoted to the training of personnel for all phases of the total literature programme.

The Commission undertook to seek resources for the Fund up to a maximum of $3,000,000 for the five-year period of the mandate. The Committee of the Fund is to be convened and the Fund launched 'as soon as firm assurances of support totalling $2,000,000 have been received'. The Commission commended the Fund to its affiliated Councils for their support:

> . . . recognizing that the creation of the Fund will entail additional expenditure for Churches and mission agencies, but believing that the importance of Christian literature in the missionary enterprise calls for this additional expenditure.

Committee 2 was concerned with '*Education for Mission and Evangelism*' in the context of the present 'new and perplexing age' and of 'the home base in every continent'. It suggested a number of considerations 'as a contribution towards gaining a new understanding of missionary education as a continuous process in the Church'.

> Education for mission is the continual discovery by its members of the nature of Christ's mission in the world, and participation in that mission.

Church members 'by their baptism . . . are committed to witness to Christ as Lord of all'; they need to 'participate in the secular struggles of our time'. The local congregation should realize that:

> God has not called it into being in order that it may be an end in itself . . . He calls it to share in the fulfilment of his mission to the world . . . The whole Church is called to mission in all six continents . . . Every Christian is called to share in the mission of the Church according to the gifts of the Holy Spirit he has received . . . He must concern himself both with those on his own doorstep and also with those at the ends of the earth, in company with the whole Church.

The Committee recommended 'a review and study of the whole concept and task of missionary education'. To this the plenary session added a specific reference to theological education.

Committee 3 considered '*Laymen in World Mission*'. Convinced that the main burden of the task of witness to the secular world and across national and confessional frontiers has to be borne by Christian laymen, and observing that laymen 'are crossing these frontiers in steadily increasing numbers for the purpose of secular employment', the Committee affirmed:

> . . . the necessity to provide Christian laymen serving abroad, through the churches in both their homeland and the host countries, with as much help as possible as they prepare themselves for witness.

The Committee expressed the judgment that the C.W.M.E. and the missionary agencies must concern themselves 'more seriously . . . with the dimension of witness in the world', particularly in connection with their plans for programmes of education for mission and evangelism. It noted with gratitude the work of the World Council of Churches Secretariat for the Service of Laymen Abroad and made suggestions for its work. It recommended that:

> . . . those laymen who go abroad with clear Christian convictions and a desire to share in the mission of the Church require something more than the orientation with which the Secretariat for the Service of Laymen Abroad is already concerned. They need to be helped to understand the witness within the secular sphere that can only be given by laymen who have crossed national, cultural and religious frontiers. The Committee therefore recommends that the staff should give further study to the form and content of such training and be ready to offer assistance in setting up suitable courses.

It recommended that Churches should be encouraged to set up local:

> . . .'encounter groups' . . . to bind together laymen wishing to make a united Christian witness in particular secular situations irrespective of their nationality or denomination.

The way in which 'regular contact between Christian laymen abroad and some link up of "encounter groups" ' may develop in the future required further study.

Committee 4 on '*Joint Action for Mission*' reviewing its meaning as it had been discussed since the New Delhi Assembly and particularly in the East Asia 'Situation Conferences':

> . . . noted that it has been understood to imply: that the Churches within an area, together with their related missionary agencies

survey, in the light of God's total calling to mission in that place, the needs and opportunities confronting them and the total resources available. The area involved should be of such a size and character, and the Churches therein should have such a degree of mutual trust and confidence, as to make possible effective action; this process of survey to be followed by a consultation of the Churches and mission bodies, aimed at securing real and effective re-deployment of resources in the light of agreed goals; thereafter the Churches to implement the findings of the consultation in definite action.

The Committee faced 'the formidable barriers to Joint Action for Mission', considered whether it was 'really possible without having reached actual church union and agreed that it was, given flexibility in its definition', affirmed that 'the effective dissemination and vigorous promotion of the idea . . . is . . . imperative' and suggested ways of doing this, noted some 'hopeful approaches to joint action', examined the various regions of the world 'to discern areas of particular promise or difficulty' and 'concluded that in every region these are real possibilities . . . Joint action is as important in the West as elsewhere'. Its report ends thus:

As we remember God's concern for his mission in the world, we look in faith for spontaneous response in many different places and in many different ways to God's calling to this next step in obedience. We believe he is leading his people along this path: the response to his leading will appear not merely in our programmes but in the initiative taken by 'all in each place'.

Committee 5 had the task of examining the 'Structure and Relationships' of the C.W.M.E. Noting that 'the C.W.M.E. is concerned with the furtherance of the Gospel in all six continents', it made suggestions concerning the relationship of organizations concerned with home mission and evangelism to the Commission. It recommended that 'the Staff in consultation with the Missionary Councils establish ways by which the major concerns of the Division can be shared with the missionary agencies', and that 'the Division should encourage the holding of situation conferences dealing with the problems of particular areas involving all the Churches in those areas together with representatives of related mission agencies'. The Commission in plenary session accepted these two sections of the Committee's report in principle, but referred them to the Divisional Committee to work out after consultation with affiliated Councils. Committee 5 commented on the financial support of national Councils; authorized the Divisional Committee to review the staffing arrangements as between the three offices in Geneva, London and New York; reviewed the relationships with the Division of Inter-Church Aid, Refugee and World Service; commended staff visits to national Councils, suggesting subjects to be discussed, and called attention to certain points concerned with the review of the structure of the W.C.C. as a whole.

In addition to these five committees, a nominating committee prepared nominations for the various Committees of the Commission. The list of members of Committees as approved by the Commission may be found in the Minutes of the meeting. This Committee also considered matters concerned with staff appointments.

Note should perhaps be made of the fact that to economize the use of available time, certain activities of the Commission were selected for major attention by committees at this meeting, other activities having been recently considered in special consultations or committees. The work of the Department of Missionary Studies (within the Division of Studies but intimately related to and financed by the C.W.M.E.) was reported on in the Director's Report, but was not made the subject of committee discussion, since the lines of its present work were already determined and a meeting of its working committee will be held in 1964. The foregoing summary therefore represents the work of the Committees at the Mexico Meeting, not a survey of the total activity of the C.W.M.E.

from

THE COMMISSION
ON WORLD MISSION AND EVANGELISM
OF THE WORLD COUNCIL OF CHURCHES

MEMBERS of the Commission on World Mission and Evangelism of the World Council of Churches, meeting in Mexico City in December 1963, and representing churches, Christian councils and mission agencies throughout the world, send this message to their fellow Christians in all the world. We have been concerned with 'God's Mission and Our Task' and with the witness of the whole Church of Jesus Christ to the whole Gospel of Christ to all men, whatever their race or nation, faith or lack of faith. We are constrained by a fresh awareness of the love of God for all men to send this message.

1. Our world is changing faster than it has ever done before. New patterns of life are taking form for the whole of mankind. In this revolutionary change, science and technology play a decisive part. This means two things: it makes possible for masses of people greater freedom, greater security, more leisure and a more truly human life; but it poses a great question—is technology to be the servant of man or his master? It is a question of life and death for the world.

2. We who know the God of the Bible know that the growing dominion of man over nature is the gift of God, but also that it is a trust to be exercised in responsibility to him. God's Lordship is the sole security for man's freedom.

3. Knowing this:

   a. We affirm that this world is God's world. The very turbulence of contemporary life is a product of man's response, either in obedience or disobedience to the living God. Men may not know this. They may ignore it. But the fact remains that God is Lord not only of creation but also of history. What is happening in the world of our time is under the hand of God, even when men do not acknowledge him. We are called to a sustained effort to understand the secular world and to discern the will of God in it. This means seeking to know what is in accordance with his purpose and what is under his judgment. Thus we rejoice in all the possibilities for fuller life now open to men, but we affirm that man is only free in God's service, and if he refuses that service he will become the slave of other powers and will end in destroying himself.

b. We affirm that the God whose world this is has revealed himself in Jesus Christ. He who is head of the Church is Lord of all. His is the name above every name. His love is for all mankind. He has died and risen again for all. Therefore we can go to men of other faiths or to men of none in humility and confidence, for the Gospel we preach is the account of what God has done and still does for all men. All men have the right to know this, and those who do know it are committed to making it known. No one, and least of all Christians, can hold that it does not matter what men believe as long as they believe something. The ultimate issue in human life is precisely who God is, and this we know in Jesus Christ. Christian witness does not rest on any kind of superiority in Christians; it rests wholly on the commission from the Christ, who came for all men, to make him known to all. Mission is the test of faith.

c. We affirm that all Christians are called to go forward in this task together. We believe that the time has now come when we must move onwards to common planning and joint action. The fact that Christ is not divided must be made unmistakably plain in the very structure of missionary work. Our present forms of missionary organization do not openly manifest that fact; they often conceal it. The far-reaching consequences for all churches must be faced.

d. We thus affirm that this missionary task is one and demands unity. It is one because the Gospel is one. It is one because in all countries the Churches face the same essential task. It is one because every Christian congregation in all the world is called to show the love of God in Christ, in witness and service to the world at its doors. It demands unity because it is obedience to one Lord, and because we cannot effectively witness to the secularized or to the non-Christian world if we are isolated from one another. We need the gifts God has given to each Church for the witness of the whole Church.

e. We affirm that this inevitably means crossing frontiers. This is true of the Christian missionary, who leaves one culture and one nation to go to people of other cultures to proclaim the Gospel of Christ. Moreover, there is an increasing number of men and women who go to other countries than their own, as Christians, in commerce and industry, or in the professions or government service. This is a two-way traffic, and all such people need the prayerful support of the congregations from which they go out.

But there are other frontiers we need to cross: the Christian congregation must recognize that God sends it into the secular world. Christians must take their part in it—in office, factory, school and farm, and in the struggle for peace and a just order in social and racial relationships. In this task they must seek the power of the Holy Spirit to bear witness, by word and by life, to the reality of the living God, in whatever ways are open to them.

4. We therefore affirm that this missionary movement now involves Christians in all six continents and in all lands. It must be the common witness of the whole Church, bringing the whole Gospel to the whole world. We do not yet see all the changes this demands; but we go forward in faith. God's purpose still stands: to sum up all things in Christ. In this hope we dedicate ourselves anew to his mission in the spirit of unity and in humble dependence upon our living Lord.

STATEMENT
TO
THE MEMBERS OF THE COMMISSION
AND THE YOUTH DEPARTMENT
OF THE WORLD COUNCIL OF CHURCHES

WE, fifteen youth delegates coming from six continents of the world, have had the privilege of participating in this historic first meeting of the Commission on World Mission and Evangelism.

This conference has been valuable to us in many respects. Through the regular Bible studies we have been helped to a deeper understanding of the Gospel we believe. Through the plenary lectures our vision has been broadened about our world which is caught up in social revolution. Through the work of the Sections we gained insight about the mission of the Church in the secular world, in our neighbourhoods, across national and confessional frontiers, and to men of other faiths. Through the Committees we have gained an appreciation of the practical and organizational problems that are being faced by the missionary movement today, and some of the ways that are being found to overcome them.

We express our thanks to God for the opportunity of attending, for the insight and understanding we have gained of the missionary task confronting us, and for the glimpse we have received of the unity of the Church.

This conference has made us realize with new force the urgency and compulsion for evangelism and world mission. As Christian young people we are part of the whole world in which we live, and we have a responsible mission in this world. We must enter into the struggles of our time and work against misery, hunger, social injustice, racial hatred and political tyranny. There are great opportunities for Christian witness in secular organizations such as labour unions, student movements, political parties, etc., as well as in any job we hold. We realize that this will be difficult but we consider this to be our obedience to the Lord's will.

It has become clear to us that this work must be done ecumenically. We recognize an unwillingness of many Christian youth to be associated with divided and splintered missionary enterprises. We feel deeply the hopelessness of a divided witness. We must move forward on several fronts.

1. We recognize the mission of the Church as involving not just clergy and professional church workers. In fact we see the real evangelistic thrust into today's world coming through committed laymen and we therefore regret that there were so few laymen involved in this conference. We urge that every effort be made to involve laymen more fully in the work of the Commission.

2. We recognize that a large number of people, especially youth, throughout the world believe in secular ideologies, or live by practical atheism. Therefore we feel that more attention should have been given at this conference to the problem of communication of Christian faith to such people. This should be a matter of study by the Departments of Evangelism and of Missionary Studies.

3. We are grateful for the promise of a new era in the missionary enterprise through 'Joint Action for Mission'. We are convinced that joint action between denominations is essential. However, we have heard many church conferences making statements and expounding pious platitudes, but little real change has resulted. We urge Churches and mission agencies to translate the decisions at Mexico City into action. We especially commend for joint action the ministry on the university campus and other youth ministries. We call Christian youth to be ready to launch out into such united enterprises for Christian witness.

4. In many parts of the world there exists a deep gulf between youth and the established Church. There also exist conflicts between generations. Both are a threat to the mission and unity of the Church. We request our elders, as well as our own generation, to recognize this and to work towards a dynamic community within the Church.

5. As Christian young people we share certain aspirations. We want to be actively involved in the secular world. We know that many are prepared to engage themselves fully in the processes of social change needed to renew our society and nations. We want to be human. We know that many young people are willing to serve the

world in need in our own home countries and elsewhere. We believe that in these and other ways the Spirit of God is leading the youth of our time to new missionary tasks. We urge the Churches to provide us with new forms of worship and fellowship, which will give us the nurture to fulfil these aspirations and new tasks.

6. We affirm that Christian youth are full members of the Church, and as such should assume full responsibility in its life and mission. We rejoice in the fact that we have been able to participate in all aspects of this conference and express our views. We do hope that more such opportunities will be provided for youth, for their effective participation in the life of the Church at local, national and international levels.

7. We feel that the great world to be won today is the world of youth. Youth form the majority of the world's population. We feel that the Churches must take seriously their mission to youth, and remind the youth of the Churches that they must carry the brunt of this task, as Christian youth are the best evangelists among youth. We urge youth to give themselves wholly where God is working to heal human lives, and to realize both the witnessing dimension of service as well as our Christian calling to express in words the reason for our servanthood.

We know that we do not stand alone in these convictions. We also know that the way ahead of us is rough and difficult but we are confident because we have the promise of him who declared, 'Lo, I am with you always.'

Key

(A)—Adviser (O)— Observer
(G)—Guest (S)—Staff
(M)—Member (Y)—Youth Delegate

* At the time of the meeting the address of the World Council of Churches and all the offices therein was 17 route de Malagnou, Geneva, Switzerland. Since then all these offices have moved to 150 route de Ferney, Geneva, 20, Switzerland.

Abraham, Mr O. C. (Y)
Theological Seminary,
University of Dubuque,
Dubuque, Iowa, U.S.A.

Student

Mar Thoma Syrian Church of Malabar

Aharonian, Rev. Hovhannes P. (M)
Near East School of Theology,
P.O. Box 235,
Beirut, Lebanon.

Principal

Armenian Evangelical Church

Ahumada-Barona, Mr J. José (Y)
Carbera 40, No. 22–F–45,
Bogotá, Colombia.

Albrecht, Miss Madelyn (S)
723 Vermont Avenue,
Saginaw, Michigan, U.S.A.

Missionary

American Baptist Convention

Altmann, Mr Walter (Y)
Caixa Postal 14,
São Leopoldo,
Rio Grande do Sul, Brazil.

Student

Lutheran Church of Brazil

Anderson, Miss Leila W. (O)
600 Lexington Avenue,
New York, 22, N.Y., U.S.A.

Executive, International Division,
Y.W.C.A. of U.S.A.

Protestant Episcopal Church

Appel, M. le pasteur André (A)
47 rue de Clichy,
Paris, 9, France.

Gen. Sec., Federation of Protestant
Churches of France

Lutheran

Arrastia, Rev. Cecilio (M)
Committee on Co-operation in
Latin America of the
N.C.C.C.U.S.A.,
475 Riverside Drive (6th floor),
New York, N.Y., 10027, U.S.A.

*United Presbyterian Church in the
U.S.A.*

Athanasius, Bishop Thomas Mar (M)
Mar Thoma Church,
Tiruvella, Kerala State, India.

Missionary Bishop

Mar Thoma Syrian Church of Malabar

Ayson, Rev. Inocencio M. (M)
San Estaban, Ilocos Sur,
Philippines.

District Superintendent

Methodist Church

Baëta, Rev. Dr Christian G. (M)
The University of Ghana,
Legon, via Accra, Ghana.

Head of Dept. of Religions

Presbyterian Church of Ghana

Baez-Camargo, Prof. Gonzalo (O)
Ave Nevado 133,
Mexico, 13, D.F., Mexico.

Bible Translator

Methodist Church

Barrueta, Rev. German Wissar (G)
Carrillo Puerto 660,
Mexico, 17, D.F., Mexico.

Pastor

Assemblies of God

Barton, Mr William E. (M)
Friends House, Euston Road,
London, N.W.1, England.

Gen. Sec., Friends Service Council

Society of Friends

Bennett, Rev. Reginald M. (M)
40 St. Clair Avenue E.,
Toronto, 7, Ont., Canada.

Canadian Council of Churches,
Exec. Sec., Dept. of Overseas Mission

*Baptist Convention of Ontario &
Quebec*

Benson, Rev. Paul (O)
Apartado 8086,
Mexico, 1, D.F., Mexico.

Sec., Student Christian Movement

Lutheran

Benson, Mrs Paul (S)
Apartado 8086,
Mexico, 1, D.F., Mexico.

Lutheran

Berkhof, Professor Hendrikus (M)
Julianalaan 18,
Oegstgeest, Holland.

Professor of Systematic Theology

Netherlands Reformed Church

Blake, Rev. Dr Eugene Carson (M)
510 Witherspoon Building,
Philadelphia, 7, Pa., U.S.A.

Stated Clerk of the Gen. Assembly

*United Presbyterian Church in the
U.S.A.*

Blanco, Rev. José Perez (Y)
Virtudes 152,
Habana, Cuba.

Council of Evangelical Churches,
Pastor

Methodist Church

Blauw, Dr Johannes (A)
Beyerincklaan 8,
Hilversum, Holland.

Professor of Religions

Reformed Churches in the Netherlands

Bliss, Dr Kathleen (M)
69 Great Peter Street,
London, S.W.1, England.

Gen. Sec., Church of England Board
of Education

Church of England

Bonzon, Pasteur Charles (M)
102 Boulevard Arago,
Paris, 14, France.

Director, Société des Missions
Evangéliques de Paris

Boyens, Rev. Armin (S)
World Council of Churches,*
Geneva, Switzerland.

Evangelical Church in Germany

Brash, Rev. Alan A. (M)
P.O. Box 297,
Christchurch, C.I.,
New Zealand.

Presbyterian Church of New Zealand

Braulio, Miss Ana Ines   (S)
   Inter-American University,
   San Germán, Puerto Rico.

   University Professor

   United Presbyterian

Brennecke, Dr Gerhard B. R.   (M)
   Georgenkirchstrasse 70,
   Berlin, N.O. 18, Germany.

   Director, Berlin Mission and
   Council of Churches for
   Ecumenical Missions

   Evangelical Church in Germany

Brown, Rev. Basil   (M)
   P.O. Box 2846,
   Cape Town, South Africa.

   Sec., Christian Council of South
   Africa

   Congregational Union of South Africa

Brown, Mrs Porter   (M)
   475 Riverside Drive (Room 1436),
   New York, N.Y., 10027, U.S.A.

   Gen. Sec., Woman's Division of
   Christian Service of the Board of
   Missions of the Methodist Church

   Methodist Church

Buchanan, Miss Wendy Gay   (S)
   475 Riverside Drive (Room 439),
   New York, N.Y., 10027, U.S.A.

   Methodist Church

Buteyn, Rev. John E.   (M)
   475 Riverside Drive (Room 1833),
   New York, N.Y., 10027, U.S.A.

   Area Sec., Bd. of World Missions

   Reformed Church in America

Calvo, Mr Samuel F.   (Y)
   Apartado 8,
   Guadalupe, San José,
   Costa Rica.

   Pastor

   Methodist Church of Costa Rica

Carleton, Rev. Dr Alford   (M)
   475 Riverside Drive (16th floor),
   New York, N.Y., 10027, U.S.A.

   Exec. Vice-President, United Church
   Board for World Ministries

   United Church of Christ

Carlson, Rev. Paul R.   (S)
   475 Riverside Drive (Room 1003),
   New York, N.Y., 10027, U.S.A.

   Pastor

   *United Presbyterian Church in the
   U.S.A.*

Carpenter, Dr George W.   (S)
   D.W.M.E./W.C.C.,
   475 Riverside Drive (Room 440),
   New York, N.Y., 10027, U.S.A.

   American Baptist Convention

Castillo-Cárdenas, Rev. Gonzalo (M)
   Apartado Aéreo 14–650,
   Bogotá, D.E., Colombia.

   Exec. Sec., Committee on Presbyterian Co-operation in Latin America

   Presbyterian Church

Castro, Rev. Emilio   (M)
   San José 1457,
   Montevideo, Uruguay.

   Pastor

   Methodist Church

Cerna, Miss Eglantina   (Y)
   Baptist College,
   Santa Ana, El Salvador.

   Teacher

   Baptist

Chandran, Rev. J. Russell   (M)
   17 Miller's Road,
   Bangalore, 6, India.

   Principal, United Theological
   College

   Church of South India

Chavez Campos, Rev. Enrique   (M)
Calle Pena 1103,
Casilla 2,
Curico, Chile.

Pastor & Superintendent

Pentecostal Church of Chile

Chikomo, Rev. Herbert   (M)
P.O. Box 8406, Causeway,
Salisbury, S. Rhodesia.

Sec., Christian Council of S.
Rhodesia

Methodist Church

Chiu, Rev. Ban It   (S)
World Council of Churches,★
Geneva, Switzerland.

*Church of England in Australia &
Tasmania*

Clemente Vazquez, Pbro. Abel   (G)
Apartado Postal 31430,
Mexico, 20, D.F., Mexico.

Presbyterian Church of Mexico

Conerly, Rev. Robert   (S)
Apartado Postal 117 bis,
Mexico, 1, D.F., Mexico

Cooke, Dr Leslie E.   (S)
D.I.C.A.R.W.S.,
World Council of Churches,★
Geneva, Switzerland.

*Congregational Union of England &
Wales*

Cram, Mr George   (Y)
4815 Grand Boulevard,
Montreal, Quebec, Canada.

Cramer, Miss Christina P.   (S)
475 Riverside Drive (Room 930),
New York, N.Y., 10027, U.S.A.

Swiss Reformed Church

Daniel, Rev. Harry   (A)
St Mark's Cathedral,
Mahātma Gandhi Road,
Bangalore, India.

Presbyter

Church of South India

Davis, Rev. Canon Alfred H.   (M)
600 Jarvis Street,
Toronto 5, Ontario, Canada.

Gen. Sec., Dept. of Missions

Anglican Church of Canada

de Ballester, Very Rev. Archi-   (G)
mandrite Dr Paul
c/o Real Consulado de Grecia,
Plaza de la Republica 9–105,
Mexico, D.F., Mexico

Orthodox

de Sainz, Mrs Esther M.   (M)
Santo Domingo 2260,
Barracas, Buenos Aires,
Argentina.

Staff, Union Theological Seminary

Methodist Church

de Silva, Rev. Lynn   (A)
490/5 Havelock Road,
Wellawatte, Colombo, 6,
Ceylon.

Director, Christian Institute of
Buddhist Studies

Methodist Church

Dickhaut, Miss Olivia   (S)
Sanatorio Palmore,
Chihuahua, Chih., Mexico.

Missionary

Methodist Church

Diehl, Dr Carl-Gustav   (M)
Kungsgatan 28,
Uppsala, Sweden.

Gen. Sec., Church of Sweden Mission

Church of Sweden

Divas, Mr L. Armando   (S)
475 Riverside Drive (Room 655),
New York, N.Y., 10027, U.S.A.

*United Presbyterian Church in the
U.S.A.*

Dominice, Mlle Clermonde   (S)
4 rue des Cèdres,
Geneva, Switzerland.

Swiss Reformed Church

Dorman, Rev. Harry G., Jr. (M)
P.O. Box 235,
Beirut, Lebanon.
Exec. Sec., Near East Christian
Council
*United Presbyterian Church in the
U.S.A.*

Duerksen, Rev. Martin (G)
Mennonite Central Committee,
Casilla de Correo 166,
Asunción, Paraguay.

Edgar, Rev. James E. (O)
World Alliance of Y.M.C.A.'s,
37 Quai Wilson,
Geneva, Switzerland.
Presbyterian

Eichele, Bishop Erich Karl (M)
Gänsheidestrasse 4,
7000 Stuttgart—1,
West Germany.
Evangelical Church in Germany

Ekollo, Pastor Thomas (A)
B.P. 38,
Douala-Deido,
Cameroun.
School Manager
Evangelical Church of Cameroun

Engel, Rev. Frank (M)
C.E.N.E.F. Centre,
511 Kent Street (3rd floor),
Sydney, N.S.W., Australia.
Gen. Sec., National Missionary
Council of Australia
Presbyterian Church of Australia

Erb, Rev. Dr Earl S. (M)
231 Madison Avenue,
New York, 16, N.Y., U.S.A.
Exec. Sec., Board of World Mission
Lutheran Church in America

Fagley, Dr Richard M. (S)
Commission of the Churches
on International Affairs,
297 Park Avenue, South,
New York, 10, N.Y., U.S.A.
United Church of Christ

Fenn, Rev. John Eric (A)
114 Langleys Road,
Selly Oak,
Birmingham, 29, England.
Professor of Christian Doctrine
Presbyterian Church of England

Flores, Mrs Vera (S)
Privada de la Antigua Taxguena 96,
Coyoacan, D.F., Zona 21, Mexico.
Methodist Church

Fransz, Miss A. L. (A)
61 Bukit Barisan, Kebajoran,
Djakarta, Indonesia.
Assoc. Gen. Sec.,
National Council of Churches
Protestant Church of Indonesia

Fry, Rev. Franklin Clark (M)
231 Madison Avenue,
New York, 16, N.Y., U.S.A.
President, Lutheran Church in
America

Gensichen, Dr Hans-Werner (S
T.E.F./D.W.M.E./W.C.C.,
Eckenerstrasse 1,
69 Heidelberg, W. Germany.
Evangelical Church in Germany

Gerard, Rev. François C. (S)
The Almonte United Church,
Almonte, Ontario, Canada.
Pastor
United Church of Canada

Germany, Rev. Dr Charles H. (S)
116, 6-chome,
Aoyama Minami-cho, Minato Ku,
Tokyo, Japan.
Missionary
Methodist Church

Gjerding, Rev. Anker (S)
D.W.M.E./W.C.C.,★
Geneva, Switzerland.
Lutheran Church in Denmark

Goertz, Mr Marc A.   (S)
World Council of Churches,*
Geneva, Switzerland.

French Reformed Church

Gonzalez y R., Rdo. Daniel   (G)
Filomeno Mata 17–214,
Mexico, 1, D.F., Mexico.

Methodist

Grais, Rev. Girgis   (M)
Second Evangelical Church,
Assiut, Egypt.

Pastor

Coptic Evangelical Church

Grant, Rev. F. C. F.   (M)
P.O. Box 403,
Accra, Ghana.

General Superintendent

Methodist Church in Ghana

Grant, Mrs Ida M. (G.C.)   (A)
10 McLaren Road,
Milton Park,
Salisbury, N.W.20, S. Rhodesia.

Missionary

United Church of Christ

Ham, Rev. Dr A.   (M)
Apartado 731,
Santiago de Cuba, Cuba.

Professor and Director of
Baptist Seminary

Baptist

Hamilton, Rev. John M.   (M)
121 George Street,
Edinburgh, 2, Scotland.

Gen. Sec., Foreign Mission
Committee

Church of Scotland

Harms, Dr Hans   (M)
Englische Planke 1,
2 Hamburg 11, W. Germany.

Director, Deutscher Evangelischer
Missions-Rat

Evangelical Church in Germany

Havea, Dr John A.   (M)
Box 25, Nuku'alofa,
Tonga Islands.

Teacher, Tupou College

Methodist Church

Hayward, Rev. V. E. W.   (S)
D.W.M.E./W.C.C.,
2 Eaton Gate,
London, S.W.1, England.

Baptist Union of Gt. Britain & Ireland

Hinojosa-T., Mr Wilfram   (Y)
Calle 16 de Julio 5939,
Casilla de Correo 86,
Cochabamba, Bolivia.

Høgsbro, Bishop Halfdan R.   (M)
Bispegaarden,
Nykøbing Falster,
Denmark.

Lutheran Church in Denmark

Honey, Rev. T. E. Floyd   (M)
85 St Clair Avenue E.,
Toronto, 7, Ontario, Canada.

Sec., Board of World Mission

United Church of Canada

Hopewell, Dr James F.   (S)
T.E.F./D.W.M.E./W.C.C.,
475 Riverside Drive (Room 1730),
New York, N.Y., 10027, U.S.A.

Protestant Episcopal Church

Hopewell, Mrs James F.   (S)
9 Summit Drive,
New City (Rockland County),
N.Y., U.S.A.

Protestant Episcopal Church

Hubble, Rev. Gwenyth   (S)
D.W.M.E./W.C.C.,
475 Riverside Drive (Room 440),
New York, N.Y., 10027, U.S.A.

Baptist Union of Gt. Britain & Ireland

Hwang, Rev. Dr C. H.   (A)
Tainan Theological College,
Tainan, Taiwan.

Principal, Tainan Theological
College

Presbyterian Church of Formosa

Itty, Mr Chirapurath I. (S)
W.C.C., Dept. on the Laity,*
Geneva, Switzerland.

Orthodox Syrian Church of the East

Jackson, Prof. Herbert (A)
3041 Broadway (at 120th Street),
New York, N.Y., 10027, U.S.A.

Director, Missionary Research
Library

American Baptist Convention

Jacob, Mr Korula (M)
Christian Council Lodge,
Nagpur, 1, India.

Exec. Sec., National Christian
Council of India

Church of South India

Johnson, Rev. E. H. (A)
63 St George Street,
Toronto, 5, Ontario, Canada.

Sec. for Overseas Missions

Presbyterian Church of Canada

Jones, Dr Irene A. (M)
475 Riverside Drive (Room 678),
New York, N.Y., 10027, U.S.A.

Assoc. Exec. Sec.,
D.F.M./N.C.C.C.U.S.A.

American Baptist Convention

Kiel, Rev. Greenfield C. (M)
Room 308,
Chr. Literature Society Bldg.,
91 Chong No. 2–Ka,
Seoul, Korea.

Gen. Sec., National Christian
Council of Korea

*Presbyterian Church in the Republic
of Korea*

Kinnear, Mrs Elizabeth (S)
D.W.M.E./W.C.C.,
475 Riverside Drive (Room 440),
New York, N.Y., 10027, U.S.A.

United Church of Christ

Kishi, Dr Chitose (M)
921–2 Chome, Saginomiya,
Nakano-Ku, Tokyo, Japan.

President, Japan Evangelical
Lutheran Church

Knight, Rev. Prof. George (O)
McCormick Theological Seminary,
800 West Belden Avenue,
Chicago, 14, Ill., U.S.A.

Professor of Old Testament

*United Presbyterian Church in the
U.S.A.*

Knipschield, Mr Donald H. (Y)
528 Walnut Street,
Anderson, Ind., U.S.A.

Writer

Church of God, Anderson, Ind.

Kotliarov, Bishop Vladimir (M)
World Council of Churches,*
Geneva, Switzerland.

Representative in Geneva of the
Moscow Patriarchate

Russian Orthodox Church

Kotto, Pasteur Jean (M)
B.P. 89,
Douala, Cameroun.

Sec. General, Evangelical Church of
the Cameroun

Kretzmann, Dr M. L. (O)
Radio Station K.F.U.O.,
801 De Mun Avenue,
St Louis, Missouri, U.S.A.

Mission Study Director

Lutheran Church, Missouri Synod

Krockert, Mr Horst (A)
General Mudra Strasse 1–3,
6503 Mainz-Kastel, W. Germany.

Co-Director, Gossner House

Evangelical Church in Germany

Kulandran, Rt. Rev. Dr S. (M)
Bishop's House,
Vaddukoddai,
Ceylon.

Church of South India

Lara-Braud, Prof. Jorge (S)
5 de Febrero 769,
Mexico, 13, D.F., Mexico.

Dean of Presbyterian Theological
Seminary

*National Presbyterian Church of
Mexico*

Latham, Rev. Robert Owen (M)
11 Carteret Street,
London, S.W.1, England.

Home Sec., London Missionary
Society

*Congregational Union of England &
Wales*

Lawson, Pasteur James S. (O)
B.P. 34,
Cotonou,
Dahomey Republic.

Associate Gen. Sec. of All Africa
Conference of Churches

Methodist Church

Lee, Rev. Eugene (S)
Apartado 9223,
Mexico, 1, D.F., Mexico.

*United Presbyterian Church in the
U.S.A.*

Leung, Dr S. C. (M)
23 Waterloo Road,
Kowloon, Hong Kong.

President, Hong Kong Christian
Council

Church of Christ in China

Liggett, Dr Thomas J. (M)
Box 426,
Rio Piedras, Puerto Rico.

President, Evangelical Seminary

Disciples of Christ

Litwiller, Rev. Juan T. N. (Chief
Casilla 52, Steward)
San Fernando, Chile.

Minister

Presbyterian Church

Lloreda, Rev. Alfonso (A)
Apartado Postal 25671,
Mexico, 12, D.F., Mexico.

Bible Translator

Presbyterian Church

Löffler, Rev. Dr Paul (S)
D.W.M.E./W.C.C.,
2 Eaton Gate,
London, S.W.1, England.

Evangelical Church in Germany

López, Prof. Mauricio A. (S)
W.C.C., Dept. on Church and
Society,*
Geneva, Switzerland.

*Evangelical Christian Church,
Argentina*

Lopez de Lara, Rev. Daniel (M)
Apartado 1373,
Mexico, 1, D.F., Mexico.

Exec. Sec., Mexico Agency of the
American Bible Society

Disciples of Christ

Lozano, Miss Enriquetha (S)
Apartado Postal 24,
Mexico, 1, D.F., Mexico.

Lutheran

Madsen, Mrs Agnes (S)
D.W.M.E./W.C.C.,
475 Riverside Drive (Room 440),
New York, N.Y., 10027, U.S.A.

Lutheran Church in Denmark

Maeda, Miss Frances (S)
U.S. Conference for the W.C.C.,
475 Riverside Drive (Room 439),
New York, N.Y., 10027, U.S.A.

*United Presbyterian Church in the
U.S.A.*

Maitimoe, Pastor D. R. (M)
Djalan Raya 1,
Bogor, Indonesia.

Pastor

Protestant Church of Indonesia

Margull, Dr Hans J. (S)
W.C.C., Dept. of Studies on
Evangelism,*
Geneva, Switzerland.

Evangelical Church in Germany

Marroquin, Rev. Antonio (G)
Apartado 4,
Guatemala City, Guatemala.

Moderator

Presbyterian Church in Guatemala

McMillan, Dr K.G. (G)
40 St Clair Avenue E.,
Toronto, 7, Ontario, Canada.

Sec., Canadian Bible Society

Presbyterian Church of Canada

Means, Dr Frank K. (O)
3806 Monument Avenue,
P.O. Box 6597,
Richmond, Virginia, U.S.A.

Sec. for Latin America of the
Foreign Mission Board

Southern Baptist Convention

Mejia, Rev. Father Jorge Maria (O)
3542 José Cubas Street,
Buenos Aires,
Argentina.

University Teacher

Roman Catholic

Meyer, Bishop Heinrich (M)
Bäckerstrasse 3–5,
Lübeck, W. Germany

Evangelical Church in Germany

Minz, Rev. Nirmal (M)
Gossner Evang. Lutheran Church,
Ranchi, Bihar, India.

Pastor

Lutheran

Molnar, Rev. Enrico C. S. (S)
Bloy House,
2249 South Harvard Blvd.,
Los Angeles, 18, Calif., U.S.A.

Canon Registrar

Protestant Episcopal Church

Moore, Mr Arthur J. (S)
475 Riverside Drive (Room 1330),
New York, N.Y., 10027, U.S.A.

Methodist Church

Moore, Dr Joseph G. (M)
815 Second Avenue,
New York, 17, N.Y., U.S.A.

Exec. Officer, Strategic Advisory
Committee

Protestant Episcopal Church

Morikawa, Rev. Dr Jitsuo (M)
611 General Armstrong Road,
King of Prussia, Pa., U.S.A.

Sec., Division of Evangelism

American Baptist Convention

Moshi, Rt. Rev. Stefano R. (M)
Lutheran Church of Northern
Tanganyika,
P.O. Box 195,
Moshi, Tanganyika.

*Lutheran Church of Northern
Tanganyika*

Muchunga, Rev. Levison (M)
P.O. Box 535,
Ndola, Northern Rhodesia.

Pastor

*United Church of Central Africa in
Rhodesia*

Müller-Krüger, Prof. Th. (A)
Evangelische Missions-Zeitschrift,
Mittelweg 143,
Hamburg, 13, W. Germany.

Study Sec., German Missionary
Council

Evangelical Church in Germany

Mukerji, Dr (Miss) Renuka (M)
The Women's Christian College,
Madras, 6, India.

Principal, the Women's Christian
College

Church of South India

Nasir, Rev. K. L.   (M)
  Theological Seminary,
  Gujranvala, West Pakistan.

  Principal, Theological Seminary

  United Presbyterian Church

Ndjock, Mr Edouard Ndjock   (Y)
  475 Riverside Drive (Room 924),
  New York, N.Y., 10027, U.S.A.

  Student

Neehall, Rev. Roy G.   (M)
  4 Francis Lau Street,
  St James,
  Port of Spain, Trinidad.

  Pastor

  Presbyterian Church

Nelioubin, Mr Boris   (S)
  World Council of Churches,★
  Geneva, Switzerland.

  Russian Orthodox Church

Newbigin, Rt. Rev. Lesslie   (S)
  D.W.M.E./W.C.C.,★
  Geneva, Switzerland

  Director, D.W.M.E.

  Church of South India

Newman, Rev. Eben Vickery   (M)
  139 Castlereagh Street,
  Sydney, N.S.W., Australia.

  Asst. Gen. Sec.,
  Dept. of Overseas Missions

  Methodist Church

Niemöller, Kirchenpräsident Dr (M)
  Martin
  Brentanostrasse 3,
  Wiesbaden, W. Germany.

  Church President

  Evangelical Church in Germany

Nieto A., Mr José   (S)
  Gante 5,
  Mexico, D.F., Mexico.

  Study Sec., Student Christian
  Movement of Mexico

  Methodist Church

Northam, Mr Frank   (S)
  World Council of Churches,★
  Geneva, Switzerland.

  Methodist Church

Nzé Engouré, M. Jean Félix   (Y)
  Eglise Evangélique du Gabon,
  B.P. 80,
  Libreville, Gabon.

  Pastor

  Evangelical Church of the Gabon

Orchard, Rev. Ronald K.   (S)
  D.W.M.E./W.C.C.,
  2 Eaton Gate,
  London, S.W.1, England.

  *Congregational Union of England &
  Wales*

Osorio, Rev. Josué   (M)
  Apartado Postal 26,
  Pachuca, Hgl., Mexico.

  District Superintendent

  Methodist Church

Parthenios, Most Rev. Coinidis Aris
                               (M)
  Piazza Santa Maria Degli Angeli,
  Tripoli, Libya.

  Metropolitan in North Africa

  Greek Orthodox Church

Potter, Rev. Philip   (M)
  25 Marylebone Road,
  London, N.W.1, England.

  Sec., for West Africa and West
  Indies, Methodist Missionary Society

  Methodist Church

Rahbar, Dr Daud   (A)
  55 Elizabeth Street,
  Hartford, 5, Conn., U.S.A.

  Assoc. Prof. of Pakistan Studies,
  Hartford Seminary Foundation

  Methodist Church

Ranson, Dr C. W.   (S)
  T.E.F./D.W.M.E./W.C.C.,
  475 Riverside Drive (Room 1730),
  New York, N.Y., 10027, U.S.A.

  Methodist Church

Regier, Rev. Dr Jon (M)
475 Riverside Drive (Room 506),
New York, N.Y., 10027, U.S.A.

Exec. Sec., Division of Home
Missions, N.C.C.C.U.S.A.

*United Presbyterian Church in the
U.S.A.*

Roberts, Rev. Earle D. (M)
Caixa Postal 133,
Campinas, São Paulo,
Brazil.

Presbyterian Church in the U.S.

Rodriguez, Rev. Antonio Rivera (M)
P.O. Box 1788,
Hato Rey, Puerto Rico.

Exec. Sec., Evangelical Council of
Puerto Rico

Roe, Rev. James M. (M)
146 Queen Victoria Street,
London, E.C.4, England.

Editorial Sec., British & Foreign
Bible Society

Church of England

Roeroe, Mr Wilhelmus A. (Y)
Pacific School of Religion,
Berkeley, 9, Calif., U.S.A.

Student

Protestant Church of Indonesia

Rossel, Rev. Jacques (M)
21 Missionstrasse,
Basel, 3, Switzerland.

President, Basel Mission

Swiss Reformed Church

Ruiz M., Bishop Alejandro (G)
16 de Septiembre 6–703,
Mexico, 1, D.F., Mexico.

Methodist Church

Sadiq, Rt. Rev. John (M)
Cathedral House,
Nagpur, 1, Maharashtra,
India.

Bishop, Chairman of D.W.M.E.

*Church of India, Pakistan,
Burma and Ceylon*

Sanchez, Miss Concepcion (S)
Rio Po 77 Col.,
Cuauhtemoc,
Mexico, 5, D.F., Mexico

Sandle, Miss Marjorie (S)
D.W.M.E./W.C.C.,★
Geneva, Switzerland.

Church of England

Sapsezian, Rev. Aharon (A)
Rua Caio Prado No. 207, Apto. 73,
São Paulo, Brazil.

Gen. Sec., Association of
Theological Seminaries in Brazil

Armenian Evangelical Church

Saucedo, Rt. Rev. José G. (G)
Calle La Otra Banda 40,
Mexico, 20, D.F., Mexico.

Episcopal Church

Sayegh, Dr. Roger (Y)
c/o M. Gabriel Habib,
B.P. 1375,
Beirut, Lebanon.

Orthodox

Schaefer, Dr John F. (M)
601 West Riverview Avenue,
Dayton, 6, Ohio, U.S.A.

Exec. Sec., Division of World
Mission

Evangelical United Brethren

Scott, Rev. Roland W. (S)
D.W.M.E./W.C.C.,★
Geneva, Switzerland.

Methodist Church

Short, Rev. Frank (M)
2 Eaton Gate,
London, S.W.1, England.

Gen. Sec., Conference of British
Missionary Societies

*Congregational Union of England &
Wales*

Sidjabat, Dr W. B. (M)
Djl. Pegangsaan Timur 27,
Djakarta, Indonesia.

Research Director

Batak Lutheran Church

Smith, Dr Eugene L. (A)
475 Riverside Drive (Room 1515),
New York, N.Y., 10027, U.S.A.

Gen. Sec., Division of World
Missions, Board of Missions;
Vice-Chairman, D.W.M.E.

Methodist Church

Smith, Dr John Coventry (M)
475 Riverside Drive (Room 929),
New York, N.Y., 10027, U.S.A.

Gen. Sec., Commission on Ecumenical Mission & Relations

*United Presbyterian Church in the
U.S.A.*

Sokolovsky, Archpriest Paul (M)
Jungmannova 9,
Prague, 1, Czechoslovakia.

International Secretary of
the Christian Peace Conference

Orthodox

Sosa, Mr Adam (M)
C. Correo 35,
Ramos Mejia,
Buenos Aires, Argentina.

Writer and Translator

Methodist Church

Sovik, Dr Arne (O)
Lutheran World Federation,
Geneva, Switzerland.

Director, Dept. of World Mission

Lutheran Church

Spike, Dr Robert W. (M)
287 Park Avenue S. (Room 62),
New York, 10, N.Y., U.S.A.

Sec. for Programme of the United
Church Board for Homeland
Ministries

United Church of Christ

Stenstrom, Rev. Arvid (M)
Tegnergatan 8,
Stockholm, Va, Sweden.

Sec., Swedish Missionary Council
and the Mission Covenant Church

Mission Covenant Church of Sweden

Stowe, Dr David M. (M)
475 Riverside Drive (Room 678),
New York, N.Y., 10027, U.S.A.

Exec. Sec., Div. of Foreign Missions,
N.C.C.C.U.S.A.

United Church of Christ

Stransky, Rev. Father Thomas F. (O)
Via dei Corridori 64,
Rome, Italy.

Staff member, Secretariat for
Promoting Christian Unity

Roman Catholic

Street, Dr T. Watson (M)
Box 330,
Nashville, 1, Tenn., U.S.A.

Exec. Sec., Board of World Missions

Presbyterian Church in the U.S.

Sutherland, Miss Carol (S)
T.E.F./D.W.M.E./W.C.C.,
475 Riverside Drive (Room 1730),
New York, N.Y., 10027, U.S.A.

*United Presbyterian Church in the
U.S.A.*

Taylor, Rev. John V. (M)
6 Salisbury Square,
London, E.C.4, England.

Gen. Sec., Church Missionary
Society

Church of England

Thimme, Dr Hans (M)
Freiligrathstrasse 16,
Bielefeld, W. Germany.

Vice-President, Evangelical Church
of Westphalia

Evangelical Church in Germany

Thomas, Mr M. M. (A)
Panavila Junction,
Thycaud,
Trivandrum, Kerala, India.

Director, Christian Institute for the
Study of Religion and Society,
Bangalore

Mar Thoma Syrian Church of Malabar

Thompson, Miss Betty (S)
U.S. Conference for the W.C.C.,
475 Riverside Drive (Room 439),
New York, N.Y., 10027, U.S.A.

Methodist Church

Thompson, Rev. D. W. (M)
25 Marylebone Road,
London, N.W.1, England.

Gen. Sec., Methodist Missionary
Society

Methodist Church

Thompson, Mr Kenneth R. (S)
370 Riverside Drive (Apt. 15–B),
New York, 25, N.Y., U.S.A.

Photographer for N.C.C.C.U.S.A.

United Church of Christ

Thurber, Rev. L. Newton (M)
Christian Centre,
2, 4-chome,
Ginza, Chuo-Ku,
Tokyo, Japan.

Assoc. Gen. Sec., National Christian
Council of Japan

*United Presbyterian Church in the
U.S.A.*

Todd, Rev. George E. (A)
475 Riverside Drive (Room 1151),
New York, N.Y., 10027, U.S.A.

Director, Dept. of Urban Church

*United Presbyterian Church in the
U.S.A.*

Toma, Rev. Vavae (S)
P.O. Box 178,
Apia, Western Samoa.

Sec., Continuation Committee
of the Pacific Council of Churches

Congregational Church in Samoa

Tonkin, Mr John Maxwell (Y)
95 Madison Avenue,
Madison, N.J., U.S.A.

Student

Methodist Church

Tornquist, Pastor Guido (O)
Apartado Aereo 20023,
Bogotá, 2, D.E., Colombia.

Director, Latin American
Committee of the Lutheran World
Federation

Lutheran Church

van Randwijck, Count Steven C. (M)
Leidsestraatweg 11,
Oegstgeest, Holland.

Sec., Mission Board

Netherlands Reformed Church

Vassao, Rev. Amantino Adorno (M)
Rua Silva Dardim 23,
Rio de Janeiro,
Guanabara, Brazil.

Presbyterian Church of Brazil

Verkuyl, Prof. Dr J. (M)
van Eeghenstraat 21,
Amsterdam, Z, Holland.

Gen. Sec., Dutch Missionary
Council

Netherlands Reformed Church

Vicedom, Prof. Georg F. (M)
Neuendettelsauer Mission,
Flurstrasse 27,
Neuendettelsau, über Ansbach,
W. Germany.

Professor of Missions & Religion

Evangelical Church in Germany

Vinay, Rev. Tullio (M)
Via Capitano Faraci 79,
Riesi (Sicilia), Italy.

Pastor

Waldensian Church

Visser 't Hooft, Rev. Dr W. A.   (S)
World Council of Churches,*
Geneva, Switzerland.

Gen. Sec., W.C.C.

Netherlands Reformed Church

Vittoz, Pasteur Pierre   (M)
5 chemin des Cèdres,
Lausanne, Switzerland.

Gen. Sec., Protestant Missions in
W. Switzerland

Reformed Church of Switzerland

Walls, Miss E. A. C.   (M)
121 George Street,
Edinburgh, 2, Scotland.

Sec., Women's Foreign Mission

Church of Scotland

Warfield, Rev. Gaither   (M)
475 Riverside Drive,
New York, N.Y., 10027, U.S.A.

Methodist Church

Webber, Rev. George W.   (M)
East Harlem Protestant Parish,
2050 Second Avenue,
New York, 29, N.Y., U.S.A.

Pastor

United Church of Christ

Wedel, Canon Theodore   (M)
Union Theological Seminary,
Broadway at 120th Street,
New York, N.Y., 10027, U.S.A.

Theological Professor

Protestant Episcopal Church

Wessels, Mr Antonie   (Y)
Wijkergouw 13,
Schellingwoude, Holland.

Student

Gereformeerd Church

Wichaidist, Rev. Charoon   (M)
14 Pramuan Road,
Bangkok, Thailand.

Gen. Sec., the Church of Christ in
Thailand

Williams, Dr Colin W.   (M)
475 Riverside Drive (Room 832),
New York, N.Y., 10027, U.S.A.

Exec. Director, Dept. of Evangelism,
N.C.C.C.U.S.A.

Methodist Church of Australasia

Winter, Mr Ralph   (S)
San Juan, Ostuncalco,
Guatemala.

Wolfensberger, Rev. G.   (S)
United Bible Societies,*
Geneva, Switzerland.

Study Secretary

Reformed Church of the Netherlands

Yamada, Rev. Chuzo   (M)
Christian Centre,
2, 4-chome, Ginza, Chuo-Ku,
Tokyo, Japan.

Gen. Sec., National Christian
Council of Japan

United Church of Christ in Japan

Yannoulatos, Deacon Anastasios   (M)
189 Hippokratous Street,
Athens (708), Greece.

Director, Inter-Orthodox
Missionary Centre 'Porefthendes'

Greek Orthodox Church

STEWARDS—

Arevalo, Mr Francisco
Centro Evangelico Unido,
Apartado Postal 117 Bis,
Mexico, 1, D.F., Mexico.

Carranza, Mr Sergio
Avenida Sur 122 No. 2652,
Mexico, 13, D.F., Mexico.

Donogho, Mr Walter
Cordoba 23A, Mexico, D.F., Mexico

Edwards, Mr Clarence
Calabar Theological College,
Half Way Tree, St Andrew,
Kingston, 10, Jamaica.

Hernandez, Mr Juan Jacobo
    Sur 124, 2760,
    Mexico, 13, D.F., Mexico.

Humphries, Miss Ray
    Sanatorio Palmore,
    Chihuahua, Chih.,
    Mexico.

Lloyd, Mr Charles L., Jr.
    Perkins School of Theology,
    Southern Methodist University,
    Dallas, 22, Texas, U.S.A.

Medillin, Mr Carlos
    Baptist Seminary,
    San Fernando 49,
    Tlalpan,
    Mexico, 22, D.F., Mexico.

Poitras, Rev. Edward
    Drew University,
    Madison, N.J., U.S.A.

Ramos, Mr Homero Job
    Baptist Seminary,
    San Fernando 49,
    Tlalpan,
    Mexico, 22, D.F., Mexico.

Velez, Mr José S.
    Baptist Seminary,
    San Fernando 49,
    Tlalpan,
    Mexico, 22, D.F., Mexico.

Waugh, Mr Winston
    Calabar Theological College,
    Half Way Tree, St Andrew,
    Kingston, 10, Jamaica.

ACKNOWLEDGMENTS

WE are grateful to all the authors, publishers and other organizations concerned for permission to use extracts from their publications.

The quotations from the Bible, unless otherwise stated, are taken from the Authorized Version. Those taken from *The Revised Standard Version of the Bible*, copyrighted 1946 and 1952, are used with the permission of Thomas Nelson and Sons Ltd., and those from the *New English Bible, New Testament*, copyright 1961, are used by permission of Oxford and Cambridge University Presses.